CONT1

Jim Shea – The Myth, The Legend

For years, I was Jim Shea's colleague and pod-mate. We got along just fine, alerting each other to office gossip and free food in other departments as well as the daily lament about traffic, politics and the sorry state of journalism. It was an easygoing relationship.

Inevitably, when I met people at parties and revealed that I was a journalist at The Hartford Courant, people would grab my arm and practically shout: "Ohmygod, doyouknow JIM SHEA? He's hissssterical. My husband and I fight over the Saturday paper to see who gets to read him first."

I'd smile politely. Yes, of course I knew Jim Shea, I'd say. I actually sit across from him.

"GET.OUT!," they'd bark, emphatically. "George, honey, listen to this – this woman sits across from Jim Shea EVERY DAY....can you imagine? You have the best job in the world."

The next time I went to work, I'd squint a little at Jim and try to see him that way.

I'd peer over the mauve divider, looking for "hisssterical." But there'd be Jim, drinking his coffee one cup at a time, just like the rest of us, mumbling lines that sometimes made it to the legal pad, sometimes didn't. On occasion, he'd lean back in his chair, prop his white and green Adidas on the edge of the desk and stare out the window. Rinse, repeat.... all day... except for the lunch break, when he'd return from the cafeteria with a small carton of milk to pour over his cereal. Not much to work with there. At precisely 4:50 p.m. every day, he'd get up, toss the legal pad on the desk, shrug into his jacket and take his leave with a casual "See ya."

But you can't dine out on that version of Jim Shea, the hard-working reporter who writes, rewrites and revises until he has stuffed every ounce of humor he can into a 12-inch column. So, I do what Jim does in his writing – I tell people what they want to hear and what is true for me as a reader. I say: "When I read Jims' columns, I think he's, like, the funniest man on the planet. I cry from laughing so hard. I read parts of it out loud to anyone in hearing distance. He's just hisssterical."

Enjoy.

Naedine J. Hazell
Editor, The Hartford Courant

CHAPTER 1

MAYBE IT'S JUST ME

This kind of stuff happens to everyone, right?

Pillow Talk At 38,000 Feet

I'm coming back from vacation, and I have my Delta-supplied pillow tucked between my armrest and the side of the plane. At some point, I decide to take a nap. But when I look for my pillow, it's gone. I look around and eventually see this old guy in the seat behind me zonked out on two pillows, his and mine.

I decide to wait until the guy wakes up to ask for my pillow back, but the guy doesn't wake up. Two, three hours go by, and the guy doesn't move a muscle. I know this because I am using the mirror from my wife's compact to watch him.

At about the four-hour mark, I get out of my seat and ask to borrow the compact again, at which point my wife asks what for, and I say I'm going to hold the mirror under the guy's nose because I think he might be dead.

My wife says if he is dead, do you really want to use that pillow? And I say not particularly, but I want the pillow back because it's not the pillow, it's the principle. And she says why don't I just ask the flight attendant for another pillow?

So I ask the flight attendant for another pillow, and she asks what happened to my original pillow, and I explain to her how it was between my seat and the side of the plane and how the dead guy behind me stole it.

She takes a close look at the dead guy but doesn't seem to be all that concerned with his condition, probably because, if he is dead, Delta will save a bag of peanuts. Then she says to me that she's sorry, but the policy is only one pillow per passenger.

If that's the policy, I say to her, then how come the dead guy has two pillows, and I don't have one.

She says that's not her concern, and I say it should be her concern because she is the keeper of the Delta pillows and, as such, has a responsibility to enforce the one-man, one-pillow rule.

I'm getting a little hot at this point, and she flashes me that I-can-have-this-plane-diverted-and-you-led-off-in-handcuffs look.

This is the last thing I want – we haven't had the snack yet – so I back off and offer a compromise: Snatch one of the pillows from under the dead guy's head, and give it to me, and we'll be even-Steven without violating the sacred one-man, one-pillow law.

She says she can't do that and walks away. Now I'm fuming. Let me borrow your pillow for a second, I say to my wife, and she asks for what, and I say so I can go hold it over the dead guy's face just in case he isn't dead.

We're midway into our landing descent when I feel something hitting the back of my arm, and I look down and see my pillow being put back from where it was stolen. Turns out, the dead guy wasn't dead after all.

You have no idea how disappointing I find this.

Misheard Lyrics

Did you ever see that "Friends" episode in which Phoebe thinks the words to the song "Tiny Dancer" go: "Hold me closer, Tony Danza"?

Everybody has mangled lyrics like this in their repertory.

One of the classics is a line from "Purple Haze." Instead of "'scuse me while I kiss the sky," it is often misheard as "'scuse me while I kiss this guy."

I mean, that's a pretty big difference message-wise. Usually, though, mishears are harmless. Take the song "Whiter Shade of Pale." Does it really matter if you are belting out, "We skipped the light fandango" or, as a friend of mine used to croon, "We skip a life and dangle"? I think not.

Nor do I think it is any big deal that some people went around for years thinking the name of the song was "Wider Shade of Pale," by a group called Poco Harlem. So shoot me.

Most of the time the lyrics we devise make sense on some level. For example:

"My Country 'Tis of Thee."
My country, 'tis of thee, sweet land of liberty, of thee I sing;
Land where my fathers died, land where the Pilgrims cried.
(Come on, wouldn't you have had a crying jag or two if you were a Pilgrim?)

"The Easter Parade"
On the avenue, Fifth Avenue, the photographers will snap us,
And you'll find that you're in the roto gray fur.
(What do I know about fashion?)

Although I have committed lyrics-cide on songs across a musical spectrum, I seem to be particularly prone to refining the story line in Christmas carols.

"Silent Night"
Silent night, holy night,
All is calm, all is bright
Round the old virgin mother and child.
(I'm thinking being in close proximity to nuns at the time I learned this carol influenced my interpretation here.)

"The First Noel"
The first Noel, the angels did say,
Was to frighten poor shepherds in fields as they lay;
In fields where they lay, sleeping with sheep.
(Hey, if you get your jollies scaring shepherds, fine. But as far as what shepherds and sheep do in the privacy of their fields, that's their own business.)

"Winter Wonderland"
Later on we'll perspire,
As we dream by the fire.
(I don't know, you just came in from a walk; you have a heavy sweater on, big fire going; all seems to tie together.)

If you don't mind, I'd like to close with a sing-along. We'll begin with "Deck the Halls With Bowels of Holly" followed by "Hark the Hairy Angels Sing."

Hip Jeans-Buying On The Fly

If, indeed, further proof is needed that nothing is simple anymore, go shopping for jeans.

Closing on a new house is simple.

Buying a halfway decent internal organ on the black market is simple.

Getting your situation situated in a comfortable pair of basic jeans should be simple – but it ain't.

I park the car and dash into the big-box clothing store figuring it is going to take about the same amount of time to pick up a new pair of jeans as it does to grab a quart of milk.

"May I help you?" the sales clerk wants to know.

"Jeans," I say, "33-31, don't bother with a bag."

"Ok, but what type of jeans are you interested in?" she asks.

"Blue," I say.

She points me toward the Jeans Department and conveniently disappears.

The Jeans Department isn't a department as much as it is a suburb. It's huge.

There are jeans stacked along both walls, jeans piled high on counters, jeans hanging from rows of racks.

I begin exploring but quickly become lost in a faded-blue sea of strange options: Cargo. Carpenter. Baggy. Boot Cut. Low Risers. Then I spy a familiar face – Levis.

Unfortunately, the old friend turns out to be unreliable, and once again I am adrift in uncharted waters, trying to gauge the pros and consequences of such styles as Flight, Skinner, Trooper, Slouch Boot and Ozzy. Ozzy?

Eventually, I stumble across what appear to be basic jeans. But even here there are decisions to be made.

Do I want a Regular, Relaxed or Comfort fit? What I would really like is all three in one, but they don't seem to come that way.

I am trying on a pair of jeans called "501s" when I discover they feature a button fly. Mind you, as a survivor of multiple zipper-fly injuries, I am all for a safer system. But buttons, it seems to me, fail to afford one the quick and easy exit certain emergency situations demand.

Another strange thing I notice about the jeans I'm trying on is that while they are being sold as new, they are worn, faded, used. Who breaks these in, I wonder? Professionals? And what shots have they had?

Toward the end of my quest, I slip into something that is intended to be worn well down on the hips. While these jeans look all right from the front, I am aghast when I catch a rear view in the mirror.

Cheek cleavage may be alluring when flashed by red-carpet celebrities on their way into the Plumbers and Steamfitters Annual Awards show, but otherwise it's generally not an attractive look.

I know it is time to give up when I find myself standing in front of the mirror in a pair of Ozzys and fighting the urge to bite the head off a live bat.

A Loser's Diary

Dear Diary: This is going to be great. I'm going to write down all the cool and interesting things that happen to me every day. This will give me a permanent record of my life, and then whenever I want I can go back and relive all the best moments. I'm really excited. Well, talk to you tomorrow.

Monday:

Dear Diary: I got up this morning. I went to work (after I took a shower). I typed stuff. I had lunch. I came home from work. I ate. I put my dishes in the sink because the dishwasher was full. I sat down to watch television. There wasn't anything on, so I watched everything. I got tired. I went to bed (after I brushed my teeth). I got up in the middle of the night to go.

Tuesday:

Dear Diary: Nothing out of the ordinary happened today until I came home and got the mail. Right on top was the American Express bill. It made me feel nervous so I did what I usually do: I put the bill at the bottom of the mail pile and thought about something else. When I went to bed, though, I couldn't sleep because I kept thinking about the American Express bill. So I got up and opened it. That was a big mistake.

Wednesday:

Dear Diary: On my way to work today, a man in a green car flipped me the bird. So I flipped him the bird. So he flipped me the bird. So I flipped him the bird. So he flipped me the bird. So I flipped him the bird and pointed to my temple and circled my finger to indicate he was crazy. Then I got off the exit. It wasn't really my exit, but I took it anyhow so I could get him last. Na. Na. Na-Na-Na. I was late for work.

Thursday:

Dear Diary: Two things happened to me this morning that were kind of cosmic. First, I woke up not feeling well. Then I read a story in the paper about bird flu, which made me feel even worse. All day long I was pretty sure I had bird flu. As it turns out, I didn't. I've decided not to eat chicken anymore.

Friday:

Dear Diary: I went to the mall after work, and I have to say I was pretty proud of myself because I didn't take out my American Express card even once. I used Visa.

Saturday:

Dear Diary: I was going to mow the lawn and run a lot of errands, but then I didn't feel like it so I just hung around all day and read and watched sports. At night I had a couple of glasses of wine. Actually it was more than a couple of glasses, but who's counting.

Sunday:

Dear Diary: I just read all the entries from the past week and have decided it is best if we end our relationship. It's not you; it's me. I need to get a life.

A Phobia About Phobias

Phobia.

Just saying the word makes my tongue sweat.

This is because among the phobias I have, is a phobia about phobias, which is called a phobophobia, which should not be confused with a phobophobiaphobiaphobia, which is a fear of repeating yourself.

All told, there are more than 600 named phobias. I know this because I just scanned the list. And I have to say, I felt better after doing so because I realized I am not alone.

For example, I'm not the only one who is afraid of the great mole rat (zemmiphobia), rectums (proctophobia), relatives (syngenesophobia), peanut butter sticking to the roof of your mouth (arachibutyrophobia), Bolsheviks (Bolshephobia), chins (geniophobia), sitting down (kathisophobia), string (linonophobia), slime (myxophobia) and clowns (coulrophobia).

I was also pleased to learn that there are certain phobias I don't have, such as:

Ergophobia, a fear of work, which in my case is more of an aversion.

Euphobia, a fear of hearing good news, which is just an Irish thing.

And lachanophobia, a fear of vegetables. (Although homegrown produce bearing an uncanny resemblance to Richard Nixon still scares me.)

Certainly the most surprising thing I discovered while performing my phobia audit were the number of fears that have not been granted official phobia status.

Among the more common are:

Dubya-phobia – Fear of the Electoral College system.

Swoosh-phobia – Fear of sweatshops.

LaGuardia-phobia – Fear of airports.

GeorgeCostanza-phobia – Fear of losing a good parking space.

RedSox-phobia – Fear of October.

Wassup-phobia – Fear of old beer commercials.

Ctrl-Alt-Delete-phobia – Fear of Windows.

Circlingcircling-phobia – Fear of admitting you're lost.

Plumberbutt-phobia – Fear of baggy pants.

ESPN-phobia – Fear of missing a sports score.

Popdiva-phobia – Fear of bellybuttons.

Ballparkfigure-phobia – Fear of car mechanics.

PriceLine-phobia – Fear of William Shatner.

ChickenLittle-phobia – Fear of TV weathermen.

Dude-phobia – Fear of backward baseball caps.

Nestegg-phobia – Fear of checking your 401(k) balance.

BigOne-phobia – Fear of large coffee in a traffic jam.

Frieswiththat-phobia – Fear of servers wearing paper hats.

Ba-da-bing-phobia – Fear of "The Jersey Shore."

Stress Test Is Pretty Stressful Itself

A lot of people seem stressed out these days.

I may be one of them.

Here are some symptoms:

I sleep with my eyes open.

I don't go anywhere without night-vision goggles.

I get road rage backing out of the garage.

I have developed a crush on Queen Latifah.

I enjoy dressing the dog in cute little outfits.

So, am I on edge, or on the ledge?

I decided to take a stress test. It was very stressful. Some of the questions made my forehead veins turn purple. I'm not sure what the test showed. The psychologist who analyzed it has changed his phone number.

Here's a copy of my test. I tried to be honest.

Work:

Q: What do you like most about your job?
A: Calling in sick.

Q: What one aspect of your job depresses you the most?
A: Having to interact with Earthlings.

Q: How much pressure do you feel under at work?
A: I bite 10 to 15 pencils in half on an average day.

Q: If you could eliminate one thing about your job, what would it be?
A: Supervision.

Q: What would give you the most job satisfaction?
A: Getting even.

Q: Do you feel you are treated differently than co-workers?
A: Well, I'm the only one they frisk in the morning.

Personal:

Q: Are you in a long-distance relationship?
A: No, I'm between cellphone plans.

Q: Are you married?
A: Why are you nagging me?

Q: Do you have children?
A: Kind of.

Q: What are your hobbies?
A: Sometimes I dance naked in front of pets.

Q: How do you feel about aging?
A: Closer to death.

Other:

Q: Do you often feel like your brain is screaming at you?
A: I'm sorry, you'll have to speak up.

Q: Have you committed a crime in the last year?
A: Hard to say – I just filed my tax return.

Q: Do you know where you will be living a year from now?
A: Again, I'm waiting on the IRS.

Q: When someone disagrees with you, what do you think?
A: That they have a death wish.

Q: What makes you cry?
A: Warm SpaghettiOs. "Leave It to Beaver" re-runs.

Q: What kind of music do you listen to?
A: I own several of Dirge's greatest hits CDs.

Q: Are you able to say those three little words?
A: Sure: Tick. Tick. Tick.

Butter My Butt And Call Me A Biscuit

When people give you a book out of the blue, they often will explain their gift by saying something like: "When I saw this, I thought of you."

Sometimes this is a compliment, and sometimes it isn't, and sometimes you're not sure which.

I mean, among the books I've received lately are: "B Is for Botox," "How Do Men Think?" and "Go Tweet Yourself."

Most of the time these kinds of books don't live up to their titles.

"Butter My Butt and Call Me a Biscuit," a collection of country sayings, is an exception.

Most of us are probably familiar with such country-ish adages as:

"Excuses are like backsides – everybody's got one."

"Grass don't grow on a busy street."

"That food was so good, it'd make a body slap his grandma."

But when was the last time you heard somebody say:

"If your cat had kittens in the dog house, would that make 'em puppies?"

"When bugs throw a party, they don't invite the chickens."

"You couldn't find your own butt with two hands and a search warrant."

"He breathes through his nose to keep from wearin' out his teeth."

Thumbing through "Butter My Butt," I quickly got bogged down in wondering about the derivation of many sayings.

For example, "Don't give cherries to pigs or advice to fools."

Now I understand about not giving advice to fools, but what happens if you give cherries to a pig? (On second thought, maybe I don't want to know.)

Here's another one I don't get:

"Time to paint your butt white and run with the antelope." (Is this like a new sport or something?)

Or how about this:

"There ain't no difference between a hornet and yellow jacket when they're both buzzin' in your pants." (I'm not sure what this means, but let me tell you, it's no fun.)

Some of my other favorites include:

"Money thinks I'm dead."

"I ain't as good as I once was, but I'm as good once as I ever was."

"I feel like a rubber-nosed woodpecker in a petrified forest."

"You look like the dog has been keepin' you hidden under the porch."

Anyway, "Butter My Butt" is highly recommended. It will make you "feel finer than a frog's hair split four ways and sanded twice."

Master Of The Domain

Home alone.

I recently found myself in this situation for a whole week, but it wasn't because everyone went to Europe and left me behind by mistake. They left me behind on purpose.

At first, it was kind of nice living alone.

I could do anything I wanted when I wanted. No one was the boss of me but me.

I put my feet up on everything, left my clothes where they fell, piled the dishes in the sink and blasted music while I watched sports with the sound down. Every once in a while I checked my pulse to make sure I hadn't died and gone to heaven.

After a while, though, the responsibility of being solely in charge of my behavior began to weigh on me. I started nagging myself. Living alone can make you weird.

One of the things I noticed, which I kind of liked initially, was that if you left something somewhere, no one moved it. The downside, of course, was that if you left something somewhere, no one moved it.

In retrospect, I think observing this phenomena up close gave me a greater understanding of the formation of clutter at the molecular level.

Somewhere around the third day, I ran out of space in the sink and decided to transfer everything to the dishwasher. Getting the dishwasher loaded proved to be fairly easy. Starting it up was another matter.

I'm still not exactly sure how this happened, but I eventually found myself reading the directions. It was fairly unsettling.

On the other hand, laundry was no problem. At risk of sounding full of myself, I've been using the clothes washer and dryer since my early 40s and seem to be pretty much past the days when everything I put in came out pinkish and smaller.

I didn't go near the stove. Sure, the house has a lot of smoke detectors, but I figured: Why push my luck? Plus, I have yet to come upon a food product you can't microwave or make a sandwich out of.

Aside from the basic survival stuff, I found the house spooky at night. Every noise, every branch scrape against the window drew my attention. I stopped answering the phone after 9 p.m. because I was afraid I'd hear someone say, "The call's coming from inside the house."

The last couple of days being home alone got sort of lonely, even though I was surrounded by a wide circle of imaginary friends. I also got into this habit of saying everything I thought out loud, kind of like when you're driving.

More ominous still, I found myself developing a real fondness for cats, lots of cats, the more cats the better.

Fortunately, we were out of milk.

This Makes My Hair Stand On End

The Internet will take you places you never thought you would go – or want to be.

Like waxing.

I've heard of waxing the car.

I've heard of waxing poetic.

But I have to say I have never heard of waxing your back, and I was only vaguely familiar with bikini waxing.

As for something called Brazilian waxing, let me just say – yee-haw!

For those who don't know what Brazilian waxing is, Google it. I'm not about to describe the procedure here other than to note it is the scorched-earth approach to hair removal.

I will also say this: Forget water boarding: You want to make a terrorist talk, Brazilian wax him.

This journey into the wilds of hair removal began when one of my colleagues asked me if I was familiar with something called the "no-poo" movement.

I assumed it had something to do with dogs and lawns, what you might call a pet peeve of mine.

As it turns out, the poo in "no poo" is short for shampoo, and the movement involves giving up washing your hair.

"No poo" advocates –Pooponents? – believe shampooing every day strips your hair of oils, causing your scalp to produce more oil, which requires more shampooing. They maintain that if you opt out of this cycle, the condition of your hair will improve.

I have my doubts.

Any time I don't shampoo for a couple of days I end up looking like a cocker spaniel that's been hosed down with WD-40.

So . . .

From "no poo" I stumbled across back waxing, which involves pouring hot wax on the back, covering it with a cloth, and then ripping it off along with all the hair underneath. I have problems removing a Band-Aid. I'd have to be under general anesthesia to have that done.

Although back waxing is generally confined to men, some women do undergo the process, none of whom I would want to meet in a dark alley.

The same basic process employed in back-hair deforestation is also used in bikini waxing, the only major difference being a newfound ability to hit the high C at the moment of truth.

There is only one thing I can think of that would be more painful that bikini waxing.

And that, of course, would be Speed-O waxing.

Worst Of Christmas Eves...
Best Of Memories

I love Christmas Eve, although I have to say the feeling has not always been reciprocal.

There was the year the pipe burst while we were out, and I was trying to get help at 3 a.m.

Quick, what do Santa Claus and a plumber you call in the early hours of Christmas Day have in common? Right: "Ho-Ho-Ho."

Then there was the time all the oil leaked out and the car engine froze up in the middle of nowhere. And, no, we didn't have a cellphone.

The most unrequited Christmas Eve, however, was what has become known as "The Country-Song Christmas Eve."

There had been a big storm a few days before, leaving our house still without power on Christmas Eve.

To make matters worse, I was suffering the lingering effects of a stomach flu. Although things had stopped coming up, I still wasn't able to put anything down. And I certainly wasn't capable of attending my family's traditional party out of town that evening.

My wife had volunteered to stay home, but when I insisted she take my daughter and go to the party, she reluctantly agreed.

She might have been just a tad more reluctant to agree, if you ask me, but . . .

After they left for the party, I situated myself on the couch under a mound of blankets close to the fireplace. For company, I had a flashlight, battery-powered radio and the dog, who didn't exactly look thrilled about being left behind.

In a matter of minutes, I was feeling really sorry for myself. It didn't help that the batteries on the radio began to weaken, and soon the only thing I could get was some distant AM station playing countrified Christmas music.

The radio crackled and whined, and at some point the high-pitched signal got to the dog, and out of nowhere he let out a howl.

So there I was, sitting home alone, sick in the cold and dark on Christmas Eve, listening to bad country music and an unhappy dog with something less than perfect pitch.

The situation was so depressing that at some point it started to be funny. And the more I thought about my plight, the harder I laughed.

The more Christmases you collect, the more they tend to run together. For me, the worst Christmas Eve I ever spent always will be one of my best memories.

I can't speak for the dog.

CHAPTER 2

MEN

I don't defend 'em, I just try to explain 'em

Men Get Short End Of The Stick

I recently read a story detailing the pet peeves women have about the men in their lives.

It was a long story, a really long story.

"Yada-yada-yada" came to mind.

I thought about responding with a list of pet peeves men have about the women in their lives (What is this obsession with cleaning when company is coming?), but then I thought: Why not take the high road?

Why not try to address some of women's major peeves from a male perspective?

PEEVE: Men don't listen.

False. Men do listen, but there is a time and a place for listening. Women, for some reason, have never grasped that the middle of a game is not the place. Watching a game takes a tremendous level of concentration. This is especially true if you are trying to watch a game and take a nap at the same time.

PEEVE: Men don't do their fair share around the house.

Come on. Who keeps track of games and scores? Who sounds the alarm when the snack-food supply is running dangerously low? Who points out it's time to begin cooking dinner and what laundry needs to be done? Who is concerned enough about the condition of the house to go out of his way to say, "Missed a spot."

PEEVE: Men don't share feelings.

Men learn from an early age that if they share any of their innermost feelings (I find cowboys strangely attractive), their buddies will make fun of them. This is why men will only share feelings if they have been drinking beer. If a woman wants to talk about feelings with a man, she should bring along a six-pack.

PEEVE: Men don't pick up after themselves.

Although this may be true, it's not for lack of trying. For example, when a man takes off his underwear and launches a long shot toward the hamper, he is not trying to miss. Women have to understand that not even Michael Jordan shot 100 percent.

PEEVE: Men are impossible to watch TV with.

Actually, this is true. But this doesn't apply just to women. Men can't watch television with other men, either. The problem is that most men have remote Attention Deficit Disorder. The only way to watch television with a man is to first beat the remote to death with a mallet. Men have been known to watch decorating-show marathons rather than get up to change the channel.

I hope this has been helpful.

The Man Cave

Every home needs a Man Cave.

Every man needs a personal refuge, a retreat, a place to scratch, to nap, to revel in manly manliness and escape the clutches of a culture that has become overly metrosexualized. Not that there is anything wrong with that. I mean, I am bi-metrosexual myself.

What I'm saying is a man needs a space where he can put his feet up and let his jelled hair down.

Where he can leave the remote on the chair and not have to worry about finding a chick flick on the 70-inch high-definition flat-screen TV when he returns.

Where he can allow his lower digestive tract to freely, frequently, even musically express itself.

The Man Cave is more a state of mind than a specific location. It can be in the garage, the basement, the attic. It can be disguised as a home office or flaunted as a Lion's Den. The important thing is that it resides outside the care, custody and control of the woman of the house.

Women, either secretly or openly, resent the Man Cave, often complaining they have no such room of their own.

This is, of course, untrue.

Women absolutely have a little nook of their own. It's called the rest of the house. In addition, they also usually possess their own private space. Although it goes by such names as the living room or the sitting room, a more apt description is . . . the Useless Room.

The Useless Room is the overly Martha Stewart-ized one with the knickknacks, frilly curtains, impressionist paintings and incredibly uncomfortable furniture. Its other distinguishing characteristic is that it is the room no one ever uses.

Despite being the major landowner in nearly every household, women always seem to be champing at the bit to do harm to the Man Cave.

They want to de-pile, dust, rearrange, burn the recliner and call in the health department. I have no idea why. I think it has something to do with their mothers.

Any assault on the Man Cave must be resisted at all costs. Failure to secure one's sanctuary, to stand firm against any and all intrusions, will have dire consequences. And when I say dire, I mean knickknacks, frilly curtains, impressionist paintings and uncomfortable furniture.

Remember, a man's cave is his castle.

Just Where Is GPS Taking Us?

No one gets lost anymore.

Even men.

Not that there has ever been a man who has ever actually been lost.

A man may not know exactly where he is going, and he may not end up where he was supposed to be, but a man always knows where he is.

If this is confusing to you, it is probably because you are a woman.

GPS is to blame for the loss of lostness.

GPS is everywhere: cars, phones, wristwatches, bicycles. . . . This is not good.

How long will it take, one wonders, before the male's innate sense of location is forever erased from our genetic code?

Consider the evolution: In the beginning, man knew where he was going, and if he didn't know, he walked behind somebody who did.

Asking for directions came next, followed by looking at maps, pulling into the gas station, MapQuest and now GPS. Can being beamed from point A to p oint B be far behind?

OK, I admit it. I have a GPS, but as is the case with most men, it serves as more of an adviser or consultant than as a guide.

My GPS is a she. Her name is Trix, sort for Dominatrix. Trix is British. She is also very bossy.

When Trix says "turn here" what she is really saying is, "Turn here you worthless sack of motoring humanity or I will whip you on the spot with the radio antenna."

I don't know, there is just something appealing about being ordered around by a stern woman with a British accent. Maybe it's the leather pants and halter top?

Although GPS offers convenience, it does so at a human cost.

With self-serve now the standard, what happens to the lonely gas-station attendant whose remaining interaction with the public is with the wife-frazzled, hangdog husband popping in to ask (make that confirm) where such-and-such a street is?

What will replace the took-a-wrong-turn excuse when you show up intentionally late for a social engagement you really don't want to be at?

And how about those always-stimulating discussions with your spouse as you continuously circle a strange neighborhood at night in the rain:

"Admit it, you're lost."

"I know exactly where I am."

"Where are you?"

"It should be right up here."

"Let's see what Trix thinks."

Men Know How To Be Sick

As flu season lurks, the question becomes, who handles being sick better – men or women?

I'm thinking men.

Unlike women, men know how to be sick.

When a man is sick, he knows he is sick, he embraces the sickness, and he has no desire to be anything but sick.

Women have a different mindset.

When a women is sick, she denies she is sick, she ignores the symptoms, and she tries to carry on as if she is anything but sick.

This, of course, is sick.

I'm not really sure why women behave this way but I think it is linked to statements you often hear them make when they are under the weather:

"If I don't do this, who will?"

And, "it's easier to do it myself."

I'm still not entirely clear on what women mean when they say such things. I used to think it was just the delirium talking, but now I'm not so sure.

In recent years I have come to suspect that these fever-fueled ravings maybe indirectly directed at men.

What leads me to this conclusion is that I have noticed after a flu-riven woman says to a man "Who's going to do this, you?" maniacal laughter often follows. (Is it possible that when it comes to the flu, bitterness is the best medicine?)

Men have a much healthier attitude toward being sick.

At the first sign of a symptom, the average male heads immediately to the couch and does not leave this self-sanctioned ICU until the last sniffle has passed.

There is suffering, but there is no silence.

There is moaning and groaning.

There is whining and whimpering.

There is beck and calling.

As for rising up and attempting to do something because it might not otherwise get done, well, good one.

Of course, there are occasions when a male is as sick as he sounds, and there is a very simple way to tell.

Place the remote in the man's hand, and turn the station to something like "The View." If the man, after crying out in horror, lacks the strength to change the channel it is time to call the EMTs, and possibly a priest.

Women really should consider adopting the male protocol when illness strikes. It's a time-tested approach. It's effective. And it's a heck of a lot easier then stumbling around in a ratty robe doing stuff that no one cares gets done but you.

Clean Undies: A Gender Thing

It has come to my attention, and I admit relatively late in life, that women change their underwear every single day.

Surprised?

You could have knocked me over with a thong.

Not only do women do this, they do it without fail. It's like some kind of thing with them.

I mean, I'm all for hygiene and everything, but isn't this kind of overkill?

Now, I do fully understand that there are circumstances and situations and such that demand clean underwear.

If you are going to the doctor, for example, you want to be wearing clean underwear if for no other reason than if your mother found out you had done otherwise it would kill her on the spot.

While there are men who change their underwear every day, they are in the minority. They are also usually married. Interestingly, studies show that of the married men who change their underwear daily, 57 percent will even wear their wife's underwear in a pinch.

Personally, I'm not sure that behavior is healthy.

The main reason single men do not change their underwear on any kind of a regular basis is because they forget to.

If a single male does remember his underwear needs replacing, and if he has a fresh pair available, he will almost always opt for a new pair . . . unless he is really tired.

Unfortunately, single men do not, as a rule, have a supply of clean underwear on hand. This is why they are often forced to recycle.

Recycling is much more involved than simply grabbing the first pair you come across in the hamper. In fact, deciding which pair of dirty underwear to put on is almost like a competition. The judging is done in the following categories:

Aroma.

Color.

Flexibility.

Rorschach patterns.

And congeniality.

I've also heard of a talent competition, but have never witnessed it myself.

Sort of takes a lot of the ick out of going commando, doesn't it?

A Man's Kitchen:
Designed For Minimum Work

What if kitchens were designed for men?

The first thing to catch your eye would be the refrigerator.

It would be taller so that everything would be at eye level, and wider, with conveyor belts rather than shelves. There would be a small TV inside to stay abreast of game action, as well as a built-in GPS system to pinpoint the exact location of things you never can seem to find, like ketchup and sides of beef.

The stove, in contrast, would be much, much smaller and feature only one large burner, which is all you really need for frying.

To save money, there would be no oven, because the only thing men use the oven for anyway is to allow day-old pizza to cure.

There would, however, be a microwave, and it would be huge, the size of a washing machine, with enough power to zap a half-dozen frozen entrees at once, in case, you know, you're having a dinner party.

There would be three dishwashers, which would be used in rotation: one for clean dishes, one for dirty dishes and one for dishes that fall between the two extremes, like those you can just brush the crumbs off, and they're good as new.

The dishwashers would not only be used for washing but also storage because, in terms of time management, cupboards just don't make any sense.

The garbage disposal also would be king-size. It would have a 2-foot diameter hole in the middle and be capable of handling anything you put in it, from chicken bones, to cans and bottles, to car parts.

To handle bulk waste, there would be a state-of-the-art trash compactor fueled by a large but tasteful nuclear reactor. This appliance would be powerful enough to reduce one of those big green bags of refuse to something the size of a cigarette pack and, in doing so, essentially eliminate the dreaded taking-out-the-garbage chore.

The toaster would appear to be standard but would be modified to shoot slices five to six feet into the air. This would not only allow for cooling but also put some of the fun back in toasting.

A key element of the male kitchen would be the floor, which would be a smooth material that could be scraped, washed and polished by simply going over it a few times with the "Home Zamboni."

It goes without saying that there would be a giant-screen TV, and it would come with surround-sound to counter the behavior of family members who insist on holding dinner-time conversations when you're trying to watch the news.

As for furniture, I'm thinking comfort and practicality; maybe two pairs of front seats from a Lexus, which, of course, would be leather, heated, fully adjustable and come with cup holders.

Yeah, we're talking dream kitchen here.

Men And March Madness (FAQ):

What is March Madness?

March Madness is a three-week period during which men would rather watch college basketball than do anything else.

Anything else?

OK, almost anything else.

How serious an affliction is March Madness?

It kills thousands of relationships every year.

How can you tell if someone has March Madness?

They will be unable to complete a sentence without using the phrase "awesome, baby."

Speaking of Dickie V., how come he doesn't announce any March Madness games?

Because there is a God.

Are there other male behaviors associated with March Madness?

There are several, but the most common is the ability to remain motionless in a prone position for long periods of time.

How are men able to do this?

They train year-round, particularly on weekends.

Why does March Madness cause men to yell at the TV?

Everybody's a coach.

Do women have March Madness?

Mostly single women.

Why don't married women have March Madness?

They don't have to.

Is female behavior overall affected by March Madness?

That's not a good question.

Why's that?

Because you are asking a man.

Who should I be asking?

Someone who might notice.

Is there a female equivalent of March Madness?

Yes, "The View" Madness.

What is The Big Dance?

Another name for the NCAA basketball tournament.

Why do they call it The Big Dance?

Because you need to be invited.

Does anyone actually dance at The Big Dance?

Just the coaches on the sidelines.

Who invites teams to The Big Dance?

The Committee.

How does The Committee decide which teams to invite?

It uses a formula called the RPI.

The RPI?
It's kind of like the Da Vinci Code.
What are "the brackets"?
The tournament schedule arranged on a blank DNA chart.
What are "the brackets" used for?
Keeping track of winners and losers.
Is there wagering involved?
You're kidding, right?
Seriously, do people use "the brackets" for betting?
Are you wearing a wire?
Finally, is there a cure for March Madness?
Yes, you need to rest and drink plenty of fluids.
Isn't that also a symptom?
That's why March Madness is awesome, baby.

Grown-Up Men In Showers

More civilized. More sensitive. And definitely more sanitary.

I am, of course, talking about the middle-aged men's locker room.

Women, especially, may find this hard to believe.

This is because women tend to view middle-aged men as being little more than relaxed-fit versions of teenage boys.

So it kind of follows that they would see the middle-aged men's locker room as one giant testosterone-toasting, wet-towel-snapping, wind-breaking celebration of male bonding.

But that depiction is from an era when the object of exercise had more to do with punts and passes than shunts and bypasses.

These days, the purpose of exertion is simply to stair-step around a situation in which you suddenly regain consciousness, only to find a stranger has pinched off your nose and is blowing previously owned breath into your lungs.

A change one notices almost immediately upon entering the middle-aged male locker room involves personal hygiene.

There is some.

No longer do you find everyone sharing a couple of towels and a single soap on a rope.

Nor does there seem to be an over-reliance on the wall-mounted dispenser of industrial-strength body detergent, with its unnatural color and uncanny ability to disinfect, deodorize and delouse without producing so much as a solitary sud.

Grooming has also evolved.

Where once a little dab would do ya, today the average is a half-dozen interrelated hair products per head, per shower – and these are the Hair Club for Men dropouts.

Those who still sport enough hair to have 'dos, all the way down to those who have pet names for their surviving follicles, employ an additional array of gels and mousses and sprays and combs and dryers capable of producing enough heat to weld.

While these factors are major players in the transformation of the boys-to-middle-aged-men's locker room, probably the greatest agents of change are the huge ceiling-to-floor mirrors that now occupy every available inch of wall space.

Although women are accused of lingering too long in the looking glass, in truth they reflect the vanity of cloistered nuns in comparison with men.

The male and a mirror are love at first sight.

However, the attraction is more complex than simple narcissism.

It is do-it-yourself male-midlife-crisis therapy.

When a middle-aged man looks into a mirror, what he sees is a reaffirmation that he has pretty much circumvented the aging process.

Never mind that the guy staring back may bear an uncanny resemblance to

Buddha in BVDs; what the owner of the image sees is Tom Cruise lip-synching Bob Seger in "Risky Business."

Not surprisingly, this two-step with self-delusion produces a significant degree of posing and primping and preening.

Other men, for the most part, are oblivious to this behavior:

One, because they are too absorbed watching their own episode of MeTV.

And two, because they respect the doctor-patient relationship.

If I Can Make It, You Can Fake It

Faking it.

Faking what?

Faking it.

It?

You know, IT.

Oh, that it.

People fake it?

Women do.

Do men fake it?

Only very strange men.

Why are we talking about this?

Because Katie Couric was talking about it.

So?

So if Katie's talking about it, America is talking about it.

Did Katie say she faked it?

She didn't say.

I'll bet she fakes it.

Why?

Because she has to get up so early.

So why do women fake it?

Experts say there are lots of reasons.

For example?

To spare the man's ego.

Women shouldn't worry about that.

Why not?

Because men basically believe that when it comes to IT, everyone's on their own.

So you're saying the male isn't devastated if the woman doesn't achieve it?

Nah; he figures she had her chance.

So it's her own fault?

Well, you can't blame the man.

You can't?

No way. I mean, he was involved for the same two or three minutes, and he had no problem.

Can a man tell when a woman is faking it?

Yes.

Yes?

Yes! Yes! Yes!

I'm confused.

Generally speaking, men know how many yeses they're good for.

So?

So, a women starts tossing around extra yeses, she's loses credibility.

You ever see "When Harry Met Sally?"

Yeah.

You didn't find Meg Ryan's restaurant performance convincing?

Not in the slightest.

Because?

Because in real life, before she was even halfway through her yesiree-ing, the guy would already have been dead asleep.

Another reason women fake it is because sometimes it takes them too long to get to it.

Women shouldn't worry about that either.

Why not?

Because, with the obvious exception, men don't mind killing time this way.

I'm sorry, the obvious exception?

When there's a game on.

Of course.

Are there any other ways a man can tell if a woman is faking it?

Depends on how perceptive the man is.

Well, what things might a real perceptive man pick up on?

Oh, I don't know; doing her nails always makes you suspicious.

Escalating Valentine's Day Demands

Valentine's Day is always a difficult time for men.

The underlying problem is the concept of romance.

Men, given time and patience, can be trained in the basic mechanics of romance, but generally speaking, even those taught to go all gooey on cue rarely grasp the concept.

The main problem is men have trouble differentiating between romance and lust.

While women see romance as an end unto itself, men see romance as a kind of pre-game show, a form of dues-paying, a variation of no pain, no gain.

The increasing commercialization of Valentine's Day has not helped.

Whereas a mushy card, a heart-shaped box of candy and/or a bunch of flowers used to put one into scoring position, nowadays they won't even get a guy to first base.

No, to even be in the ballpark these Valentine's Days, a man must be willing to stoically endure all manner of humiliation. Like taking baths:

I don't know where or when this started, but for some reason the ultimate romantic evening now involves taking a bath together. And we're not talking utilitarian bath here – you know, with Irish Spring and dandruff shampoo. Rather, we're talking baths with oils and rose petals and flickering candles. I think I can speak for most men when I say: why not just toss a radio into the tub while you're at it.

Like the getaway:

When did Valentine's Day turn into Valentine's Weekend? Men, even the ones who might be considered romantic, are only good in short spurts. You drag a man away for two or three straight days, and all you are doing is diluting the product. The other major drawback to the getaway is that it usually involves some type of cozy bungalow place where, if they even have a television, it doesn't pick up ESPN.

Like the chick flick:

Sitting through a two-hour relationship movie is only slightly less painful for a man than having his gums scraped with a hacksaw. All movies that fall into the chick-flick genre have the same five components: crying, laughing, misunderstanding, Meg Ryan and Hugh Grant.

Like shopping for frillies:

It is one thing to thumb through the Victoria's Secret catalog; it's quite another to walk around one of their stores trying to figure out just what the various thingee-thongee things are and where they might go. I might also add that there has never been a case in which a male, left on his own in a Victoria's Secret store, has been able to resist the urge to pick up a stretchy thingee-thongee thing and try to slingshot it across the room.

Where have you gone Russell Stover?

CHAPTER 3

MEN VS. WOMEN

Women are from "The View"; Men are from ESPN

Renegotiating The Male-Female Pact

I have been reviewing the terms of a male-female contract worked out by the editors of Maxim and Cosmopolitan magazines, and I am feeling, well, hosed.

Representatives from the two publications took it upon themselves to meet at a New York bar to hammer out compromises on a wide range of common relationship issues.

So how did it go?

Let's just say that if this one-sided sellout were allowed to go unchallenged, the American male might just as well turn in his tool belt, start shaving on the week-ends and take up antiquing.

It is for this reason that I declare the Maxim-Cosmo agreement – hereafter known as the "Pantywaist Pact" – null and void and demand negotiations be reopened.

To facilitate the process, I have staked out the following male positions:

The seat: The toilet seat is not a complicated piece of equipment. It is either up, or it is down. If you find it up, put it down. If you don't notice it is up and you fall in, how is that our fault?

Feelings: You want to talk feelings with us, fine. Just be prepared to discuss such emotional subjects as our first car, the best dog we ever had and Bucky Dent's home run.

Noticing stuff: Don't expect us to notice every little thing, like you shaved your head or that you have been gone for a week. It's not all about you, you know.

Movies: We understand that we have an obligation to go to a certain number of movies that do not contain gun play, car chases or frontal nudity. The question is how many. In the spirit of compromise, it is proposed that the ratio of guy movies to chick flicks be 5, er, make that 10-1.

TV remote: In the control of anyone but a mature male, this device is only used to 10 percent of its potential. Leave it in the hands of the professionals.

Shopping: We don't shop, period. Shopping is why God invented your annoying girlfriends.

Gifts: We have no idea what you like, or what is appropriate, and we never will. So let's just cut to the bottom line here and agree on the following – cash.

Anniversaries and birthdays: Again, go out and get yourself something nice, and put our name on it.

How it makes you look: If you want to know if you look fat in something, look in the mirror. If you insist on making it a trick question – how fat does this make me look? – don't take it personally if the answer includes such comparisons as big rig, defensive tackle or double-wide.

Sundays: Sundays are sacred, particularly Sunday afternoons during football season. This is non-negotiable.

Finger-Walking Through Debris

If you had to name the two things most responsible for slowing everybody down, they would have to be:

Drivers talking on cellphones.

And women looking for stuff in their pocketbooks.

Give me a situation in which a woman has to go into her pocketbook for something – checkbook, money, a pen, glasses – and I'll show you a line.

Give me an arctic January night in a mall parking lot, and I'll show you a guy suffering from hypothermia while the custodian of a handbag rummages for a set of car keys, which as it turns out are attached to a ring the size of a basketball hoop.

You want to know what the surest sign is that you are in for a long wait? It's when you hear the words: "I've got it right here in my purse."

One of the reasons women can't ever seem to locate anything in those mobile storage facilities they lug around is because when they go looking for stuff, they don't actually look, they feel around.

I'm not saying women don't have a highly refined sense of touch, or that they can't differentiate among shades of lipstick by just feeling the tube. My point is that it takes a lot of time to finger-walk your way through the debris.

Of course, the only thing slower than a woman going through her bag looking for something is a man going through a women's bag looking for something for her.

If you are male and have half a brain – which I readily admit cuts down on the field some – you know that a women's purse is a weirdly private personal space, and nowhere you ever want to venture, even with permission.

I know anytime I have ever stuck my hand into a woman's purse, I always have experienced the same series of unsettling sensations:

It's kind of humid down there.

What's with the layer of gravel at the bottom?

Are all these tissues used?

There's got to be $100 in change.

Ouch.

Did something just breathe on my knuckle?

What's that? Ew!

Something's definitely stalking my thumb.

Run. Run.

I think I'm lost.

A good rule of thumb for men is this: Never agree to retrieve something from a woman's bag unless you own your own airport luggage X-ray system or have access to a balm-sniffing dog.

Finally, and in all seriousness, given the potential for human gridlock, we cannot continue to ignore the 500-pound knockoff Kate Spade in the middle of the room any longer. If we don't act, the pocketbooks win.

Meet Mr. And Mrs. Bickerson

Weather makes people sweat the small stuff.

"Does not."

"Does so."

Which accounts for the recent surge in bickering.

"Sez who?"

"Sez me."

Although bickering is also affected by cold, rain, snow, fog, wind and the picture-perfect day, nothing spurs quibbling for quibbling's sake like hazy, hot and humid.

"What do you know?"

"I know what I know."

In its purest form, bickering is a cross between stream-of-consciousness grousing and never having an unexpressed annoyance. It is not so much tit for tat, as it is tiff for tat. It also appears to be the preferred form of communication between married people.

Bickering is often confused with arguing.

This is understandable because both call for give-and-take between disagreeing parties (except in New York City, where it is not uncommon to encounter someone walking along the street squabbling among himself).

While arguing and bickering do share some characteristics, they are actually quite dissimilar. Arguing demands passion, purpose, perspective, scoring points. Bickering involves none of that. The important thing in bickering is not winning or losing; it is getting in the last word.

"Like I said."

"OK, then."

"Right."

"Well, fine."

Another thing that differentiates bickering from arguing is logic. There is only one explanation for those occasions in which the Bickersons' back-and-forth makes any sense: "The X Files."

"I think it's a beautiful dress."

"What do you know about dresses? You voted for Kerry."

As a general rule, the longer couples have been together, the more adept they become at bickering. In fact, those most accomplished at it are not even aware they are bickering. This is probably a good thing for the obvious reason: It gives them one less thing to bicker about.

Bickering is also contagious. You mix the Bickersons in with two or three relatively normal couples, and in a matter of minutes you will see more split hairs than in a beauty salon.

Inter-couple bickering is always a huge mistake but is often difficult to avoid. The most seasoned will sometimes seek to suck innocent bystanders into their spat. Don't bite. The minute you offer an opinion, you become fodder:

"See, she agrees with me."

"What does that prove? She's an idiot."

Anyway, if you must bicker, marriage counselors advise that you take the following precautions:

After eating, wait one hour before bickering.

Avoid bickering between 10 a.m. and 2 p.m.

And, of course, drink plenty of fluids.

Shopping Is No Vacation For A Guy

There inevitably comes a point during every summer sojourn when the unwinding male is wrenched from his repose and made to participate in a group activity for which he is decidedly ill suited.

Vacation shopping.

The unwinding male does not vacation shop. He does not voluntarily walk into stores and spend inordinate amounts of time comparing and contrasting cheesy merchandise.

Mostly this is because shopping to the unwinding male is both emotionally and physically draining, more taxing even than watching someone give birth.

But then it is important to understand that to the unwinding male, trying on a single pair of pants is a shop-until-you-drop experience.

On his best day, the unwinding male is good for maybe two stores, 5 minutes or a single purchase, whichever comes first.

Conversely, on her worst day, the fully wound female can easily go from dawn to dark, hit a couple of hundred stores and buy enough stuff to require porters.

Obviously, these respective energy levels do not make for compatible vacation-shopping companions, the major problem being this:

While one party is fully engaged in a tourist-trap tour de force, what does the other party – in the absence of a rope conveyance upon which to recline – do?

Essentially, the unwinding male is forced to choose between two roles: vassal or vagrant.

As vassal, the unwinding male follows behind at a respectable distance, looking very much like an old dog on a hot day. He has one duty and one duty only: To refrain from complaining.

While the vassal may be a sorry sight, an even sadder, more pathetic figure is the unwinding male as vagrant.

Sitting on benches, leaning on cars, standing, staring, strolling aimlessly within a perimeter so tightly defined, it could be controlled by invisible fencing, he loiters outside store entrances.

Joined in misery by other vagrants, yet very much alone, he makes no eye contact, makes no attempt at communication. But then, what is there to say?

Suddenly, bells jingle and a door opens.

A score of defeated faces turn in unison, each looking for a sign that their afternoon of rainy-day penance may finally be over.

Invariably, there is disappointment.

The fully wound female disappears into yet another store.

The vagrant shuffles down to his next lonely post.

Meanwhile, back at the over-priced cottage, waves break and roll, gulls swoop and cry, and an unoccupied hammock swings gently, lazily, tragically in a late summer breeze.

Five Wives, 29 Kids

I can't stop thinking about that polygamy guy from Utah.

Obviously this boy's family tree never forked.

But he still got convicted.

Now, I'm not a lawyer or anything, but five wives and 29 children?

What, they don't have an insanity defense in Utah?

That said, it's not the legal but the practical aspects of the arrangement that I am spending way too much time wondering about.

Like, say, in the morning. How does the polygamy guy get into the bathroom? I got one kid at home and three bathrooms, and I'm always pounding on doors.

Then there's the multiple-wife thing.

A lot of people see this as a good deal for the polygamy guy but a bad deal for his wives. I think just the opposite.

I mean, he has:

Five wives telling him to pick up after himself; five wives wanting to share the remote.

Of course, you have five wives, that means you also have five mothers-in-law.

And having five mothers-in-law is like having a 24-hour cable channel dedicated to whom your wife should have married.

Then there is the constant pressure of special occasions.

Keeping track of five birthdays, five anniversaries, five previous gifts, five sizes and five favorite colors, not to mention getting all the changing ages and romantic highlights straight is, well, kind of like asking the male brain to climb Mount Everest without oxygen.

The only thing I can figure is the polygamy guy must have a staff.

Without question, what I wonder most about is how they coordinate the marital relations thing.

From what I've read, the wives range in age from 24 to 31, which places all of them at their sexual peak.

Now, one man and five women at their sexual peak might work, if the man were, say 14, or had been governor of Arkansas.

But the polygamy guy is 52. And, trust me, when 52-year-old males fantasize about positions, the majority of the time they're not thinking about sex, they're thinking about Barcaloungers.

Still, given that he has 29 kids, you have to assume there is activity.

My theory is they use a system similar to the standard Major League Baseball pitching rotation, which means each wife would get the call, so to speak, once every five days.

The problem with this type of schedule, though, is that with four days between starts, the wives are going to be fully rested, as opposed to the polygamy guy, who is likely going to be in full arrest.

Anyway. Right now, the polygamy guy is facing up to 25 years in prison if his conviction stands and, as far as I can see, the death penalty if it doesn't.

Women's Rooms Awash In Splendor

Although men are gaining ground, we still have a long way to go to catch up with women.

I'm talking about restroom facilities.

I'm talking about the porcelain ceiling.

The difference between the average men's room and the average women's room can be summed up in a single word:

Bidet.

Now, I've never been really clear on how a bidet actually works, other than it involves some kind of Super Soaker water-pistol action.

What I do know, however, is this:

Women's rooms have bidets.

Men's rooms have …

Urinals.

I mean, just say the words:

Bidet sounds like a field of wildflowers waving in a warm breeze.

Urinal sounds like a guy with a cold clearing his throat.

Here is what the interior of a typical men's room looks like:

Along one wall are the urinals, conveniences that also serve as ashtrays, chewing-gum collection points and homes to large pink pellets.

There are also stalls, the condition of which is difficult to visualize unless you have spent time in a Turkish prison.

Sometimes there is toilet paper, but it is hard to keep it in stock because the typical grade makes it an excellent choice for sanding wood.

Other amenities include:

A liquid degreasing agent that claims to be soap.

A streaked or stained mirror that someone has recently punched.

And a dispenser that parcels out stamp-size paper towels one square at a time.

As for ventilation, let's just say that if you sent a canary in, it wouldn't last 10 seconds.

In contrast is the women's room.

Granted, I've never actually been in a women's room, but from snippets I've gathered over the years, I think I have a pretty accurate picture of the accommodations.

First off, it's big, with high ceilings, crown molding, hardwood floors, oriental rugs and chandeliers. There are also plants, fresh-cut flowers and impressionist paintings on the paneled walls.

The furniture consists mostly of couches and chairs, with a strong preference for Chippendale.

There is ample tissue paper, and it is of a quality that does not include bark.

There is scented soap in individually wrapped packages.

There is soothing New Age music.

There is a cappuccino machine.

There is an attendant/masseuse named Olga.

There are rows of tastefully decorated stalls, all of which are plush, private and soundproof. Some even have cable.

And, of course, there are the ornate marble bidets individually carved to resemble miniature Italian fountains.

Have I left anything out?

Martha Stewart's Revenge

Men don't match.

When it comes to color coordination, men understand that:

Black goes with blue.

Lime goes with gin.

And blondes go with anything.

Other than that, though, the most the average guy usually hopes for is that the stains don't clash.

Women are a different story.

Women can match jewelry to eyes, to hair, to makeup, to shades of fabric color so nuanced that the blending can only be fully appreciated with the assistance of a crime-lab microscope.

Married women are even capable of piecing together ensembles that complement their spouse's male-pattern baldness.

Normally, I don't have a problem with this.

Match and let match is what I've always said.

But now the whole thing may be getting out of hand.

I was sitting at the dinner table over the holidays when I noticed that the plates, cups, utensils, napkins, place mats, tablecloth, wife, children and dog all matched.

I, of course, was the pair of brown shoes to this tuxedo of domestic coordination.

It was at this point that I had one of those moments in which you are able to see into the future with a clarity reserved for disciples of Dionne Warwick.

The scourge began innocently enough, but then they usually do.

Diners and dining-room tables match the wallpaper, which matches rugs, which match the furniture, which matches everything else down to the dust bunnies frolicking under the beds.

Soon, houses match adjacent houses, and then all the houses on the street match.

And then streets match streets, cities match cities, counties match counties, and states match states, until everyone and everything in the country match.

Then the international matching begins, with country after country falling into lock step until the affliction reaches the breaking point, and every American's worst-case scenario is realized – we become indistinguishable from Canada.

Oh, the humanity.

Martha Stewart, of course, is to blame for all this.

Martha is the one who turned homemaking into a close-order drill.

Martha is the one who gave obsessive-compulsive behavior a good name.

Hold it, I'm having another vision:

I see Martha. She is in court. She is standing between identically dressed, identical-twin lawyers who match the judge, the sheriff and the prosecutor, who all accessorize well with the jury.

Martha is sent to prison. Everyone in prison wears orange jumpsuits, and no one looks good in orange, and only the Temptations look good in jumpsuits. So Martha may have met here, well, her match.

And that's a good thing.

The Division Of Household Labor

"You never do anything around the house."

If ever there was a declaration designed to ruin a perfectly good Saturday afternoon nap, that has to be it.

And you know what? It's dead wrong – for the obvious reason.

By taking a nap, I am doggedly confining myself to a small area, thereby not messing up larger areas that would then require more extensive cleaning.

So when you are totaling up who does how much, in fairness, should I not get credit for inactivity, it being, in essence, a form of preventative housework?

(I went to law school for nine straight days right after college. I'm still recovering.)

Anyway. I've been reading this study done by the University of Michigan about how much housework women do as opposed to men.

The report contains both good news and bad.

On the one hand, it concludes, and I quote: "U.S. husbands are doing more housework while wives are doing less."

On the other hand, the study also points out that women still do more housework than men.

The problem with these kinds of studies, of course, is that they only deal in quantity, not quality.

For example, it is estimated that 80 percent of the dirt that comes into the home can be captured on mats or rugs situated at points of entry.

So, if a man were to take charge of vacuuming these mats and rugs, he would, in effect, be responsible for collecting 80 percent of the dirt that enters the home.

But how long would this take, a few minutes at most? Which is all the housework time he would be credited with.

Conversely, a woman who vacuumed the entire home gets credit for hours of housework, even though she was only accounting for 20 percent of the dirt.

Thus, the male is being penalized for being efficient, while the female is being rewarded for inefficiency.

Another thing that is unfair when computing the division of household labor is the question of just what constitutes housework.

Is not mowing the lawn the same as vacuuming the carpet?

Is not changing the oil the same as changing the child?

Is wearing the same underwear for two or three days not the same as doing laundry?

What about those times during the middle of the night when a suspicious noise downstairs must be checked? Should a man not be fairly compensated for the time he spends worrying until his wife returns?

In summation, I say the only logical conclusion to be drawn here is that the American male is not being afforded his due. But then what else is new?

The defense rests.

Don't Take It Out On Me

I find myself a victim of misplaced anger.

Since writing a column comparing men's and women's rooms, I have become a whipping boy for disgruntled females on the go.

And what did I do to deserve this? I simply wrote what I believed to be the truth:

That what's considered pampering in the men's room is potable water, while the average women's room routinely features such amenities as oriental rugs, chandeliers, Chippendale furniture, masseuses and cappuccino machines.

Many women took exception to this depiction.

Some said mean things.

I was called clueless, stupid, annoying and "typical" (whatever that means).

Although varied, the hostile reaction did contain a common thread, a complaint that women often have to endure long lines when frequenting public restrooms.

Now, while I am willing to concede that my description of the average women's room may not have been entirely accurate – I've never actually been in a women's room – I feel it is grossly unfair to blame me for long lines.

Nor do I feel it is fair to suggest that the lines are the fault of the men who design public facilities.

As I see it, the three main reasons for most women's room bottlenecks are:

The Buddy System: Women rarely go it alone. Given a choice, they prefer pairs or packs. Why? I suspect so they will have someone to talk to while waiting in line. Eliminate those who are just along for a good time, and the queue will be reduced by at least 50 percent.

Attire: More often than not, women are not dressed for speed. Hidden beneath the simple dress are interlocking layers of complex belts and snaps and hosiery and thong-ee things, all of which must be dismantled and then reassembled. This is very time consuming.

Technique: Because of a design flaw, women are required to sit to heed nature's call. Unfortunately, most women would rather explode than touch down on a strange seat. As a result, when forced to use communal facilities, women hover. Hovering is not good for accuracy. And the worse the accuracy, the higher one is forced to hover, until those at the back of the line end up doing chin-ups on the door jamb.

In conclusion, let me just say that the solution to the problem of women's room's lines is not, as some of the more radical elements suggest, unisex facilities.

The superior efficiency of the men's room is not only predicated on ease of use but also on maintaining a strictly business ambience. You start adding fancy furniture and cappuccino machines, and trust me, in no time, everybody would be hovering.

A View From The Fiscal Depths

The monthly meeting of the Household Budget Committee will now come to order.

The secretary will call the roll.

Dad, don't you think you're going just a little bit overboard here?

No I don't, honey, I mean Madam Secretary. Please call the roll.

Can I go on the record as saying this is lame even for you.

Call the roll, please.

Fine. Dad.

That's Mr. Chairman, Madam Secretary.

Mr. Chairman.

Present.

Mom, I mean, Madam Treasurer.

Where's your mother?

You mean Madam Treasurer?

Where's Madam Treasurer?

She's not coming.

Did she say why?

She did.

And?

Well, to summarize, Mom says you always go mental when you talk about money, that you end up blaming her for everything, that you have no idea what anything costs, and that there's no money left to argue about anyway.

Anything else?

Oh, yeah. You're a dictator.

Unbelievable. I move your mother be fined $100 for missing the meeting.

Can we please just get this over with?

Very well, the secretary will read the minutes of the last meeting.

OK. The meeting was called to order by Chairman Mao – oops – Mr. Chairman, on Saturday morning at 9:30 by the clock in the kitchen, which is usually a little fast.

9:31 – Mom said there was no money left in the checking account, and dad got all red and had this major fit.

9:32 – When Dad's fit was over, Mom started yelling and called Dad a name, which I wrote down here, but am not allowed to say out loud.

9:33 – Dad's eyes got real wide, and this kind of azure-blue vein – I have a blouse the same color – popped up on one side of his forehead and burrowed all the way across to the other side like in that movie where the giant worms are chasing Kevin Bacon. It was freaky. I couldn't take my eyes off it.

9:34 – I asked if this would be a bad time to bring up that I need a new pair of jeans that are on sale now for $50.

9:34 – Mom and Dad both yelled shut up at the same time, which I'd like to point out is not good for my emotional development.

9:35 – Dad was so angry at Mom that when he tried to say something all that came out of his mouth was this real high-pitched whistle that made the dog bark. But what was really scary was the way Dad started to, like, foam right at the corners of his mouth.

9:36 – Mom, on the other hand, got very calm and had this real cold look in her eyes. And then she made a motion the meeting be adjourned and said to me that it would be in my best interest if I seconded the motion, so I did.

9: 37 – Meeting adjourned.

10:30 – Mom and I left for the mall, where we bought my jeans and a lot of other stuff, which I think Mom was doing for some reason other than to help keep me from being the absolutely worst-dressed kid in the school. But then I could be wrong about this, because, you know, I've never been married.

CHAPTER 4
WORK

It's not the job it's the cubicles, the bosses, the killer fungus office gnats

A Case Of Cubicalitis

I am sitting in my cubicle as I write this.

My space is but one of the 20 or so cookie-cutter blocks that make up the labyrinth that is my office.

Aside from scale ory rat's maze:

The prospect of cheese.

And an electrical grid to shock you in case you make a wrong turn.

The cubicle was invented by a man named Bob Propst in 1968. In retrospect, the only worse thing that happened in 1968 was the song "Harper Valley P.T.A." – oh, and Nixon.

You know what Propst said about his ubiquitous creation before he died? He said it was the "greatest mistake" of his life.

He also called the cubicle "monolithic insanity."

He had the insanity part right, but not the monolithic. Cubicalization has resulted in a form of bizarre group behavior – cube think – that is accepted as normal because it is efficient.

For example: You call an insurance company cube 10 times with the same question, the same cubite may give you 10 different answers – in 10 different accents. Nuts, yes, but cost-effective.

There is, of course, no personal privacy in Cubicle Nation:

You cannot take a nap without someone noticing.

You cannot talk to yourself without someone asking you to speak up.

You cannot sneeze without a chorus singing "bless you."

And let's not even get into the medley of other bodily arias from which there is no escaping responsibility.

Another thing you cannot do in the cube-o-sphere is argue with your spouse over the phone because, if you do, everyone will take your spouse's side because you are the only one they hear raising your voice and sounding like a jerk.

As a result, you get these kinds of phone conversations:

Incoming (loudly): "Did you or did you not say you were going to call the bank and get that straightened out?"

Outgoing (sweetly): "You know, dear, I don't remember ever saying that, but I'm sure I must have because you are never, ever mistaken. In fact, you're perfect."

Incoming (very loudly): "You are an irresponsible, inconsiderate, self-centered dork."

Outgoing (sweetly): "Thank you, honey. You would know more about those traits than anyone I know."

Incoming (screaming): "If you keep talking to me in that tone of voice, I swear I'm going to come down there to your crumby little cube and rip your lungs out."

Outgoing (whispering): "And I love you, too, dear. Bye now, and have a great day."

You know, what's rather remarkable is the cubicide rate isn't even higher.

When Did Experience Become A Minus?

It's a tough job market.

It's a really tough job market if you are of an age where you know the words to elevator oldies and your favorite fantasy show is "Nip/Tuck."

Apparently, people doing the hiring these day haven't gotten the memo that 60 is the new 40. To the new breed of bosses, 60 is the new Depends.

The job dilemma used to be that no one wanted to hire you because you didn't have any experience, and you couldn't get any experience because no one would hire you. Experience was everything. Now, the more experience you have, the less desirable you are.

This makes about as much sense as searching for the doctor with the most moisture behind his ears to do your brain surgery.

In reality, experience is as important as it ever was.

Are not most of the executives at the top of the world's largest corporations on AARP's mailing list? Does not the same hold true for the politicians who are running this country?

OK, bad examples.

But does it make sense for an employer to automatically eliminate a job applicant from consideration solely on the basis of mileage? Shouldn't you at least call him or her in and kick the tires?

Granted, there are some disadvantages to hiring baby-boomerish applicants, foremost among them being a tendency to talk about icky medical procedures. That said, the pluses greatly outweigh the personality quirks.

10 REASONS TO HIRE BOOMERS:

1. They already know the job, probably better than you.

2. They don't waste a lot of time texting, tweeting, surfing, e-mailing or checking Facebook.

3. They are fully awake before noon.

4. They are far less apt to come in hung over.

5. They don't call in sick unless they are actually sick, which, admittedly, is kind of unAmerican.

6. They don't gossip, mainly because they forget the juicy stuff they hear, if they can hear it at all.

7. They don't get caught up in office politics because they are where they want to be – employed.

8. They are rarely involved in office romances, thank God.

9. They don't have one eye on their job and one eye on Monster.com.

10. Finally, and most importantly Mr. and Ms. Manager, they are not out to get your job.

A Reality Checklist For Interns

The summer interns arrive – fresh-faced, brimming with enthusiasm, eager to learn – like lambs to the slaughter. Over the next several months they will, under the guise of obtaining real-world experience, be asked to perform tasks so menial that even the best colleges have not adequately prepared them.

How one survives the summer internship and lives to exaggerate the experience on the resume, depends in no small part on an ability to negotiate the office politics and personalities he or she is likely to encounter. To summer interns everywhere, we in the work world say welcome. And now, here's the lowdown on some of the people you will be working with:

THE GOSSIP: This person knows, or thinks she knows, everything about everyone and lives to tell what she has sworn not to reveal. The key to working with the gossip is to not believe or repeat anything she tells you, and to never, ever confide anything personal to her.

THE LOSER: He won't be that much older than you, but will seem kind of cool in comparison to college guys (even ones who can make beer come out of their nose). Sure, the loser may have a new car, and he may not even still live with his parents, but the question you have to ask yourself about him is this: Why, after five years, is he still in charge of making the coffee?

THE SUCKUP: Contrary to popular belief, the most effective way to identify these individuals is not by the color or condition of their noses. Sucking up has become much more sophisticated. While all suckups differ slightly in approach, they all tend to believe the boss actually knows what he is doing (a notion you will soon discover for yourself to be absurd).

THE LECH: This guy believes he is God's gift to women, and who knows, maybe he was 20 years ago. Unfortunately (for you) he thinks young women find middle-aged men such as himself irresistible. Forget subtlety in dealing with this guy. Tell him straight out that you have rules against dating men older than your father, or men who don't grow their own hair.

THE KNOW-IT-ALL: He or she will be helpful while you are still learning the ropes, but after you grasp how things are done – such as filing alphabetically – this person will get on your nerves and begin to remind you of someone you know but can't quite put your finger on. Speaking of which …

THE FATHER/MOTHER FIGURE: They will see you as the last thing you want to be seen as – a kid – and will want to smooth your way with hovering, unsolicited advice and gushing praise for the slightest evidence of competence. The best thing to do is treat these "work parents" like your real parents, and if cold indifference doesn't work go to the headphones.

THE DISGRUNTOR: These individuals take negativity to a new level. They see only the bad, rarely, if ever the good. They hate their job, the company, the boss and in short order, they will hate you.

THE DELEGATOR: If this person is put in charge of you, prepare to work long and hard because they will not only ask you to perform the job you were hired to do, but their job as well. (If this person then takes credit for the work you are doing, well, welcome to the real world.)

MR. OR MS. ANNOYING: This individual has no friends at work, the main reason being they possess the bubbly personality of a game-show contestant. Beware, they will latch onto you like a suction cup.

THE NITWIT: This guy or gal doesn't do any work when the boss is out of the office, and then can never figure out how the boss knows he or she wasn't doing anything. The real-world lesson here is that people who are forced to do your work because you aren't doing it do not suffer for long in silence.

ONE FINAL NOTE: Interns should understand that the above descriptions represent a relatively small portion of the workforce, and that the vast majority of your co-workers will probably just ignore you.

How Not To Impress The New Boss

New boss.

This can be very tricky.

Essentially, I think there are two approaches:

(A) Try to make a good first impression.

(B) Try to make no impression.

Personally, I usually go with the latter. I take this route because:

(A) I generally need at least several chances to make a passable first impression.

(B) I have come to understand there is an art to planting a big wet one on a fanny, and it should not be attempted by those lacking a natural-born, lips-on affinity for the work.

In other words, leave the sucking up to the professionals.

And just who are the pros? Surely you have seen these 9-to-5 suction cups in action:

They yes ma'am.

They can do.

They wear what the boss wears, even if it means cross dressing.

And really, what does it get them outside of a name plate and simulated wood-grain desk?

Bad hours.

Bad stomach.

Bad wardrobe.

No, when a new higher up is introduced into the workplace, the amateur's best bet is to lie low. Disappear into the underling self-preservation program and wait to see how things shake out.

The most important thing to determine is this: What kind of boss type are we talking about here:

Hands on?

Hands off?

John Gotti?

During the low-profile phase, the greatest danger to anonymity will be – The Meeting.

At The Meeting, the following two things will happen:

(A) The new boss will give a pep talk laced with war, sports and nautical metaphors.

(B) You will be invited to ask questions.

Do not take the bait.

Besides blowing your cover, no good can come from asking a question because:

If you ask a dumb question, you will be branded.

If you ask the question everyone wants to ask – How in the world did you ever get this job? – you will be branded.

One thing you should do at the meeting, however, is listen for the words "fine-tuning."

If the new boss mentions the words "fine-tuning" your first reaction should be "resume." "Fine- tuning" is boss speak for "clean house."

Eventually, the time will come when you have no choice but to interact with the new boss.

You will be nervous because, this is, after all, the person who approves the vacation schedule.

Rehearsal is key.

She will ask: Where have you been hiding?

Your best response: Who are you?

She will then point to the name plate on her simulated wood-grain desk.

You then imply you have been so absorbed in your work that you didn't even realize she had arrived. But welcome.

She will not buy this, but then that is to be expected.

This being, of course, only your first crack at making a passable impression.

Have Skills, Will Work

To: Headhunters R Us.
Subject: Career alternatives.

Dear Mr. Headhunters:

Since you contacted me, I have been doing some serious thinking about what I would like to do if I didn't do what I do now.

Right off, I'd have to say that if I could be anything I wanted, my first choice would be poet laureate. This has been my dream job ever since I first heard the words "roses are red, violets are blue."

You can ask people who know me, and they'll tell you I'm really good at rhyming stuff. You know, like somebody will say something like car, and right away I'll come back with bar. Or we'll be in a market, and the word orange will be mentioned, and I'll say … well, you get the picture.

If all the poet laureate jobs are taken, another thing I wouldn't mind being is a mentor. I could get an office downtown, and people could come in to see me, and I would tell them what's wrong with them and what they should do with their lives. Maybe I could even work with my wife, who's really, really good at this.

But just in case there are no openings in mentoring or poet laureateing, I have put together a wish list of additional jobs I wouldn't mind trying. In order, they are:

Sidekick.
Friend of the Court.
Major Player.
Senior Fellow.
Oracle.
Professor Emeritus.
Favorite Son.
Patron of the Arts.
Matinee Idol.
Confidant.
Raconteur.
Go Between.

I have to admit that one thing you were right about is that journalism does give you the skills to work in other occupations. In fact, once I started thinking about it, I was really surprised by how many other fields are open to someone like me. I mean there's …

Pundit.
Analyst.
Antagonist.
Sycophant.

WORK | 55

Informed Source.
Special Interest.
Operative.
Shadowy Figure.
Spokesperson.
Assassin.
Wretch.
Material Witness.
Moral Authority.
Insider.
Outsider.
Face in the Crowd.
Exotic Dancer (ask me about this one).

Of course, in preparing these lists, I did come across several jobs that I'm certainly qualified for but that just hold no appeal for me. They include:
Glutton for Punishment.
Player To Be Named Later.
Gofer.
Fuddy-Duddy.
Rubber Stamp.
Pooh-Bah.
Hostage.

Oh, and definitely put me down as a no for anything in the area of Whipping Boy or Sacrificial Lamb. Granted, the money and bennies are good and everything, but there just doesn't seem to be much of an upside to this kind of work.

"Working" From Home

Working" from home.

I put quotations marks around the word "working" because office-bound colleagues always do that little quotation marks thing with their fingers when someone asks where you are.

Granted, there was a time when the only difference between "working" from home and taking a day off was not having to make the dying-breath phone call to the boss to inform him that the folks running your life-support systems feel you should remain in the ICU until at least tomorrow.

These days, however, "working" from home has gone legit. Technology has made it possible, the price of oil and the financial crisis have made it a necessity. (Have you tried to get a mortgage on a tank of gas lately?)

While "working" from home has a cushy ring to it, the reality is that it can be very challenging. Here are just a few of the obstacles you have to overcome:

Paranoia: Sure, they gave you permission to work from home but did they do this because they trust you, or because they know you are incapable of producing without direct supervision and they are out to get you? (A third possibility is that you have some really disgusting habits and they like to keep you away from the office as much as possible.)

Guilt: Given that you are "working" from home and not slaving away in the sweat pods, there is often an urge to do more. Usually this passes, but it is a concern.

Distractions: During the course of an average day "working" at home at least a hundred things crop up that are more important than what you are supposed to be doing: Write the report or water the plants? Make sales calls or rearrange the sock drawer? Engage in strategic thinking or clip problem toenails? All difficult choices.

Gossip: When you are out of the office, you are out of the loop, which means two things. One, you are not up on the latest office gossip. And, two, because you are not there, you are the latest office gossip.

Appearance: A major attraction of "working" from home is not having to get all dressed or hygiened-up. Thus, it is all too easy to find your ratty-robed, funky self sitting at the kitchen table in the late afternoon wondering why your kids don't bring their friends around anymore.

Bottom line: A bad day "working" from home is still better than a good day in the office.

Office Killer Fungus Gnats

It has been a harrowing two weeks.

The office has been under siege by tiny flying bugs.

At first, everyone assumed they were fruit flies. Fruit-fly infestations are fairly common around here, where almost everyone eats at their desks all the time.

Usually when there is fruit-fly activity, it can be traced to any one of a number of usual suspects and the 3-week-old banana they forgot under a stack of coffee-stained press releases.

This time, however, the source could not be readily located, so a PBI (Private Bug Investigator) was brought in.

After a thorough investigation, which I believe included the deployment of tiny little leg-hold traps, the PBI declared that we did not have a fruit-fly problem, we had a fungus-gnat problem.

You can imagine the horror, the panic.

I'm not exactly sure how you tell a fruit fly from a fungus gnat, but I think it has something to do with facial hair.

To counter the fungus-gnat encampment, the PBI set out a bunch of orange traps containing a liquid that smelled a lot like vinegar. You know how they say you can catch more flies with honey than vinegar? Apparently, this isn't the case.

After all the traps were deployed, the insect encounters increased dramatically. What I think happened is that the fungus gnats were joined by fruit flies drawn to the vinegar-smelling traps.

I say this because fruit flies are also attracted to the half-eaten salads people lose under stacks of coffee-stained press releases, although I do have to say it has been my observation that fruit flies do prefer balsamic to regular vinegar.

Anyway, the fungus gnats – I think fungus gnats are the ones with the goatees – started to become more and more aggressive. This led to fears that they were becoming Africanized, morphing into killer fungus gnats.

Soon rumors were spreading that the Africanized killer fungus gnats had trapped an intern in one of the stairwells and covered her in so much fungi that she looked like a loaf of month-old bread.

The report turned out not to be true, the intern's greenish hue owing to the two-week old Cobb salad she had absentmindedly nibbled on while working.

There has not been a fruit fly or fungus gnat sighting in several days now, but the fear lingers.

Press 17 For More Options

Good morning.

And welcome to Jim Shea's column.

Press 1 if you are reading this column at the breakfast table.

Press 2 if you are reading this column with your pants gathered around your ankles.

Thank you.

Because your readership is very important to us, we ask that you remain with this column until the next humorous observation becomes available.

Due to the volume of readers currently scouring this column in search of the next humorous observation, the estimated waiting time is about:

Three-Hundred-Words.

Press 3 if you would like to hear "Otis' Greatest Hits" while you wait.

Press 4 if you are surprised to be hearing "Otis Elevator's Greatest Hits."

Press 5 if you would rather shower with Larry King than listen to this music.

Press 6 for more options.

Thank you.

Press 7 if you would like to speak to Jim Shea's boss about this column.

Press 8 if you would like to speak to Jim Shea's mother about this column.

Thank you.

We're sorry, but due to the volume of calls, neither Jim Shea's boss nor mother is available at this time.

Press 9 to leave a detailed, profanity-laced message.

Press 10 to cancel your subscription.

Press 11 to renounce your citizenship.

Thank you.

We're sorry, but due to the volume of calls, those voice-mail boxes are full. You may either try again later, or:

Press 12 for more options.

Thank you.

The approximate waiting time for the next humorous observation is:

Two-Hundred-Words.

Press 13 if you have developed irritated bowel syndrome while waiting.

Press 14 if you have forgotten why you were calling.

Press 15 if you have expired.

If you have expired, you may Press 0 at any time and an operator will assist you.

Thank you.

We're sorry, but due to the volume of calls, all of our operators are busy at this time helping other dead or dying readers.

You may either try again later, or:

Press 16 for more options.

Thank you.

The approximate waiting time for the next humorous observation is: One-Hundred-Words.

We're sorry, but due to the sheer number of people searching this column for any humorous observations, we are unable to assist anyone at this time. Please hang up and try again next Saturday.

Thank you.

And remember, your readership is very important to us ...

Advice From The Managed

I don't like the word manager.

I guess it's because I don't like the idea of being managed, unless, of course, I'm tiring in the late innings.

I mention this because I have been reading a book aimed at helping managers become executives.

These kinds of books always crack me up because the people who write them have no clue what's really going on in cubicle nation.

Probably the major thing they fail to understand is that we, the managees, are fully aware of how they, the manager du jours, are trying to manipulate us.

We've seen it all before, lots of times. Managers are short-timers. The bad ones get canned. The really bad ones get promoted. (I'm not sure what happens to the good ones. Nobody is.)

Anyway, in the interest of helping aspiring mangers get to that big corner office in the sky, here is an appraisal of some of your favorite techniques:

Schmoozing.

(Yeah, we love it when you ask about the kids we don't have.)

One-on-one meetings.

(Fine, as long as you don't keep glancing at your watch the whole time, and while you are at it, don't read your e-mail, make phone calls, eat, doze off or do any personal-hygiene stuff.)

Department-wide meetings.

(Contrary to belief, we kind of like these. They allow us to catch up on our sleep and do personal-hygiene stuff.)

Probing, constantly trying to assess morale.

(What you need to understand is that we are not all that subtle. For example, if after work you find all four of your car tires flat, things are not going well.)

Telling us about yourself.

(Save your breath. We've already read your file.)

Attempting to be self-effacing, laughing at yourself.

(Might as well join the club.)

Public criticism and power trips.

(Granted, this does motivate us – to go out to the parking lot and check your tire pressure.)

Lavishing praise.

(Unless it comes with a raise, forget it. We know the only reason you say nice things is to get us to do more work.)

Jumping in to help out when things get busy.

(Don't, it just makes more work for us.)

Finally, a word or two about enthusiasm.

(There is nothing that annoys us more than a peppy, sunny, upbeat manager. A key thing to remember is this: You see work as a stepping stone. We see work as a millstone. So give it a rest.)

The Office Christmas Party

From: Human Resources
To: All employees
Subject: Office Christmas Party

As you are aware, our annual holiday party was held last evening, and I don't think it is an exaggeration to say that things got totally out of hand.

As you know, this is the first year we allowed "spirits" at the party, and I can assure you it will certainly be the last.

Although final lab results are pending, preliminary analysis of the punch-bowl contents indicates the presence of both grain alcohol and space-shuttle fuel.

Now, I assume you are all aware that surveillance tapes from last night's party not only are circulating on YouTube this morning but the DVDs are also available for purchase (and apparently doing quite well).

Particularly popular seems to be the "Season's Greetings" message spelled out in bare bottoms pressed against the windows on the 11th and 12th floors.

Speaking of which, the employee "Code of Conduct" is quite specific regarding workplace comportment.

Even under the most liberal of interpretations it is clear that the enticing of female co-workers to reveal certain body parts in exchange for necklaces strung with pitted olives is unacceptable.

This next matter is a bit delicate but nonetheless needs to be addressed.

I am speaking, of course, of the numerous amorous entanglements that were noted throughout the course of the evening.

Putting aside the matter of personal fidelity, it is important for employees to remember that the supply closets are for supplies; the restrooms are designated Men's and Women's for a reason; and rug burns do not fall under workers' compensation.

Regarding the question of judicial powers that were claimed by some during the party, be advised that department heads are not vested with the authority to join couples in temporary matrimony or annul pre-existing relationships.

In conclusion, I want to briefly touch upon a few other issues:

First off, no one in upper management found the faxed photocopies of your bare buttocks amusing.

Second, the bowling with cheese balls was not a hit with the janitorial staff.

And third, having the dog – no matter how much he seemed to be enjoying himself – swimming around in the punch bowl to keep it stirred is not sitting well with the ASPCA.

Finally, for those of you who passed out and awakened to find your heads glued to various surfaces, be advised that we are making progress and are hopeful all of you will be freed by the end of the business day.

That said, have a Merry Christmas and a Happy Hanukkah.

CHAPTER 5

TEENAGERS

The care, feeding, and understanding of this strange breed

Teens Aren't Morning People

More and more school systems are looking into starting high school classes later.

They hope that by doing this, students will show up in a state loosely approximating consciousness.

At the moment, this is not the case.

Ask any teacher who has a first-period class, and they will tell you that not only do high school students fail to participate at 7:30 a.m., they don't even blink.

In fact, the absence of visible life signs is so prevalent that many teachers consider a pulse rate above 60 to be a passing grade.

As for interaction, let's just say that on a good day, it is not uncommon to hear a teacher bragging to her colleagues:

"You know, I really connected with them today. There had to be five or six different times when I asked a question, and someone grunted. I'll tell you, it was exhilarating. It reminded me of why I got into teaching. ''

The reason teenagers make the comatose look perky in comparison is because they have the sleep smarts of bats.

For many of them, their first clue that it may be time for bed is the appearance of this big yellow thing on the horizon.

Parents know their teenagers don't get enough sleep, but they have no control over it. This is because the average parent is not able to stay up late enough to tell their teenager to go to bed.

In most households, the interaction between parents and teenagers after about 9:30 p.m. is probably best described as bladders passing in the night.

Experts say the reason teenagers can't fall asleep at a reasonable hour is because their body clocks are in a different time zone than the rest of civilization.

I don't buy this.

I think the main reason they don't go to bed is because their body clocks get too wound up by all the cellphoning, texting, surfing, TV-watching, music-listening – and occasional spurts of homework-doing.

Another thing with which I disagree is the idea of starting school later.

If you change the high school schedule, then you have to adjust the parents' schedules as well as the schedules of just about everyone else in town.

This seems like an awful lot of trouble for a mere hour or so of extra sleep. I suppose you could start classes at 1 p.m., but that would mean teachers' having to teach in the late afternoon, when their biological clocks are sounding the nap alarm.

Parents and educators might try looking into something a lot less complicated and probably a lot more effective than later start times – enforced boredom.

You want teenagers to go to bed at a decent hour? Get yourself some timers, and shut off the electricity at 11 p.m.

Lie Like A Rug About Your Past

Kids are always interested in their parents' past.

This presents an interesting dilemma for Mom and Dad: How much do you lie?

There are two schools of thought on this, three if you count, "Go ask your mother."

One school, the new school, believes you should never lie to your kids about anything. In most cases, these parents had really dull lives.

The other school, the old school, believes you should lie to your kids about any subject that has the potential to one day be tossed back in your face as follows: "But you did it when you were my age."

Personally, I'm a cross between the old school and "Go ask your mother."

Not only do I think it's OK to lie to your kids, I don't think you can begin lying to them early enough.

For example:

"Mom, where did I come from?"

"My stomach, honey."

"But how did I get into your stomach?"

Now, this is where it gets tricky. You can go with:

"The stork put you there, dear."

Or, you can go with the truth:

"As I recall, your father and I were drinking wine, and I believe there was a chandelier involved."

Lying often not only directly benefits the parent but the child as well.

Say little Johnny comes home from his Little League game after having struck out five times and asks: "Dad, did you ever strike out five times in one game when you were a kid?"

With option a.), you lie: "Sure, son, lots of times."

With option b.), you respond: "I gotta tell you, son, I wasn't very good, but I was way better than you."

The real moments of truth arrive when your kids become teenagers and begin asking questions like: "Mom, how old were you when you lost your virginity?"

What do you say?

a.) "Why, right about when I was your age, dear."

b.) "Let me think, either 29 or 30."

Or your teenage son asks about trying marijuana.

a.) "Absolutely not. Once I saw the movie 'Reefer Madness,' I was scared straight."

b.) You're kidding me. My nickname in college was Bong.

Dishonesty is always the best policy, and that's no lie.

How To Talk To A Teenager

Some parents think teenagers are the most difficult group with which to hold anything resembling a back-and-forth conversation.

Others maintain that the standard six-panel door is actually less responsive.

Personally, I think it's kind of a toss-up. From my experience, the only real difference between talking to a teenager and talking to the standard six-panel door is the knob.

Regardless of which side you come down on, though, there is no getting away from the fact that at some point teenagers take a vow of silence.

This, however, does not mean all communication must stop. It is still possible for parents to communicate with their teens if they adhere to the following guidelines:

1.) Do not attempt to talk to your teenagers when they are eating, on the computer, listening to music, talking on the phone, getting ready to go out, showering, doing their hair, have just gotten up or are staring off into space.

2.) Never make sustained eye contact with your teenagers. They view this as an attempt on your part to look inside their skulls for information.

3.) Boil down the message you wish to convey to your teenager. A good rule of thumb is the dog-of-average-intelligence test. To wit: Sit. Speak. Fetch. No. Bad. And: Get your feet off the furniture.

4.) Learn to listen, and to interpret your teenager's responses:

One grunt – I heard what you said.

Two grunts – Stop nagging me.

5.) Avoid trying to converse with your teenagers in their bedroom. You will just start yelling at them and this could cause an avalanche.

6.) Also avoid asking your teenager questions that can be answered yes or no.

Poor question – That pile of laundry in your closet, is something dead under it?

Better question – That dead thing under the pile of laundry in your closet, what state of decomposition is it in?

7.) Buy a portable defibrillator. This could very well save your life in the event your teenager initiates a conversation.

8.) If you need information from your teenagers, don't ask them yourself. Rather, have one of their friend's parents ask for you.

9.) Consider the following topics off the conversational agenda: hygiene, diet, grades, homework, relationships, friends, attire, hair ('do and color), location and symbolism of tattoos.

10.) No matter the level of exasperation, never ask rhetorical questions such as:

Am I talking to myself?

What am I, an idiot?

Finally, remember the key to communicating with teenagers is patience. Eventually they will come around. Inevitably, they will need money and/or want to use the car.

Additional Drivers' Ed For Teenagers

The time has come to make it harder for teenagers to get a driver's license.

Right now, all an aspiring driver has to do is obtain a learner's permit, take several thousand hours of instruction and pass stringent written and driving tests.

This is not enough.

While the current curriculum may prepare new drivers for the road, it does little to address the budding fender-bender's relationship with the family car.

To correct this oversight, the following law is herewith proposed:

That before any teenager of any species be granted said license to drive in any state, he or she must pass the following test, which shall be administered and graded by his or her said parents, who shall have the final say in any and all disputes and determine what shall constitute a satisfactory or unsatisfactory score.

Sit up straight; no talking; do not roll your eyes on your neighbor's paper. You may begin.

General

Who owns the family car?

Who does not own the family car?

If there is a scheduling conflict, who always gets to drive the family car?

Can you think of any circumstances in which your parents should have access to the family car on a Saturday night?

Define the word scratch.

Define the word dent.

Multiple choice

If the car lacks this, it will not run:
1. Gas.
2. A CD player.

Exxon, Getty, Gulf and Mobil are all:
1. Spelled wrong.
2. Gas stations.

If the car is making a strange sound, you should:
1. Bring it right home but not tell anyone.
2. Turn up the radio.

If you get into an accident, which word will best define your father's reaction:
1. Bonkers.
2. Ballistic.

Trick Questions

If you are supposed to be home by 11 p.m., what time do you have to be home?

If there are five seats in the family car, what is its maximum capacity?

When is it inappropriate to purchase gas with your own money?

True or False

Speed limit signs are only advisory.

High mileage increases a car's value.

It is more important to make eye contact with your friends than with the $50,000 car in front of you.

Accidents don't affect insurance rates.

Your mother is a good **driver** because she can apply makeup while in motion.

Essay

You are driving down the road when the car in front of you stops suddenly. You have time to do only one of the following two things: hit the brakes, or change the station to get rid of a really icky song that has just come on. What do you do?

High Schoolers, Showers And Gym Don't Mix

Count me among those who were not shocked to find out that most high school students don't take a shower after gym class. I would have been surprised to discover otherwise.

This is not to suggest I have ever been left woozy by a malodorous pack of teenagers fresh from dodge ball.

Rather, my views have been shaped by shards of knowledge. I know a little bit about teenagers, and I know a little bit about showers, and I know a little bit about high schools. And from what I know, the combination has absolutely no chance whatsoever of coexisting.

At home, the average teenager spends more time in the shower than mildew. I have no idea what they do in there once the bathroom door locks and the water begins to splash. And I'm not sure I want to know.

I've always assumed that the rising steam tends to lull them into some kind of warm-and-fuzzy state from which escape in under a half-hour is physically impossible. Or maybe it's just a zit thing?

Either way, this time frame does not blend particularly well into the average high school schedule, where classes are generally in the 40- to 45-minute range.

As things stand right now, a student would have just enough time to get undressed, put on a gym uniform, get undressed, take a shower, and then get dressed again. This is probably not the type of workout the President's Council on Physical Fitness has in mind.

Even if all this could be accomplished in 45 minutes, what about the drying and styling of hair, which can be a very involved process? And how about time for the re-insertion of jewelry?

At the bare minimum, for mandatory showers in high school to work from a time perspective, each gym class would have to be followed by at least one full period devoted to remodeling. In my mind, this is not only impractical, it's almost unpatriotic.

Americans come from a proud and gamey tradition. The colonists didn't have showers in their homes. The settlers didn't include bathtubs in their covered wagons. And how many cowboys wore a different outfit every day? No, back in the funky old days, folks were content to smell like folks.

Then, of course, Madison Avenue came along and convinced everyone that it was infinitely more desirable to go about stinking of aged leather or ripe lime.

The fragrance police have so completely taken over our underarms that many people take showers before participating in activities that ordinarily are followed by showers: weight training, aerobics, sauna.

Now I'm not saying that everyone should stop using soap and start going around smelling like soup. But a little less musk and a little more au naturel wouldn't hurt.

Getting back to this high schoolers sans shower situation, I think it actually has an upside.

For one thing, it saves the beleaguered taxpayer a lot of money. Anybody out there want to pick up the hot-water tab for 1,000 or so teenagers to shower each week? And how about the potential brown out all those revved-up hairdryers would create?

There is also a potential public health benefit.

At certain times of the year in Connecticut, people have to slather on all manner of chemical concoctions to keep virus-carrying mosquitoes at bay. To date, no mosquitoes with the potentially deadly eastern equine encephalitis have been found in these parts. Coincidence?

Just to be safe, I say we throw open the doors of our high schools right after gym class in late summer and early fall, and send the more pungent pupils out to do some preventive fumigating. For extra credit, of course.

It's All About Communication

Can you tell me again what we're doing at Starbucks?

I thought we could have a conversation.

About what?

Whatever. I just think we should try to communicate more.

Ohmygod, like don't take this personally or anything, but this is like my worst nightmare.

Geez, why would I take that personally?

Look, I'm 15, girls my age don't have conversations with their fathers, especially in public.

Especially in public?

Yeah, I mean what if someone were to see us, I could be labeled a security risk.

Security risk? I'm not even sure what high school you go to.

Can we please just get this over with?

All right, so, how's school?

OK.

Could you be a little more expansive?

OK, school's OK, like in, you know, OK. OK?

OK. And how are you doing in school?

I can't say.

You mean you don't know how you're doing?

No, I mean I can't say – state law.

State law?

Yeah, a student's grades cannot be revealed without a court order. It's a privacy issue.

That may be true, but I don't think it applies to the student's parents.

Obviously we interpret the statute differently.

Hmmm.

So, how's your friend Mallory?

Why do you want to know?

Just curious.

Is this off the record?

Er, uh, sure if you want it to be.

Off the record – she's OK.

Good to hear. Good to hear. Say, what's Mallory's last name, anyhow?

I can't say.

State law?

Not that I know of.

Then why can't you ...

I don't know her last name.

But isn't she your best friend?

Yeah.

Didn't you just make her your sole heir?
And your point is?
How can you not know her last name?
It has never come up.
Does she know your last name?
You'd have to ask her.
Off the record, of course.
Of course.
Um, Dad, can I ask you a question?
Shoot.
Have you been listening to my phone calls?
Absolutely not.
Well one of my friends said she distinctly heard a click the other night.
I may have been trying to make a call.
Can't you check with me before you pick up the land phone?
Don't you have your own cell phone?
Sure, but I have to leave that open for texts, tweets, calls and e-mails.
Aren't you being a little unfair here?
Unfair? Do you have any idea what it could do to me socially if word got out that my home phone is compromised?
I can't even begin to imagine.
So, is there anything else you want to talk about?
No, I think we've covered it all.

Packing The Kid Off To College

If you are going to be taking a kid to college for the first time, I offer this advice:

Call your local Teamsters chapter right now, and see about reserving a crew.

If you are sending a son off, a four-man team, provided they are motivated, should do the trick.

If you are sending a daughter off, think 18-wheelers, forklifts and a convoy.

I speak from experience.

Last year at about this time, I began nagging my daughter about packing for school.

She would be sharing a room the size of a walk-in closet with three other girls, and there wasn't going to be much room for anything but essentials.

I was assured everything was under control.

In retrospect, my mistake was in not agreeing on a working definition of the word "essentials."

When I went off to college, my two gym bags worth of "essentials" included:

Toothbrush, deodorant, pillow case, sheet, towel, some jeans, some shirts, some shoes and socks, a coat, a few sweaters, a sweatshirt, a couple of albums (Beatles and Stones), and a month's supply of underwear (four pair).

And, of course, a No. 2 pencil.

In contrast, among my daughter's "essentials" were:

Three pillows.

Multiple bedding changes.

A half-dozen towels.

The cosmetics aisle from CVS.

Computer, printer, speakers, TV, desk chair, lamps, fan, rug, bookcase, telecommunication equipment.

Boxes of clothes.

Boxes of footwear.

Boxes of medical supplies.

Enough food to support an Everest expedition indefinitely.

And a No. 2 pencil (my contribution).

Well, you can imagine my surprise when on the big day I began to pack the old SUV for the trip.

It proved to be quite a challenge, but one that I was up to.

In fact, had my wife not gotten uncooperative at the last minute and refused to be lashed to the roof-rack for a couple of hours, I would have had the car loaded and ready to go on the first try.

As it turned out, we were able to squeeze everything in by permanently altering the shape of some objects, and weeding out certain items, such as the boyfriend.

I could at this point recount the trip itself (always check the knots) and the subsequent portage of cargo up three flights of stairs (the dorm elevator is never working) but my intent here is to be constructive rather than work through a recurring nightmare.

So, as I said, think about a good-size truck and an army of stumpy-armed guys named Bruno.

Oh, and one other thing. You know the term empty nest? It has nothing to do with the absent offspring. It refers to what the house looks like when you get home.

Negotiating With A New Teenager

I say to the kid:
"Mow the lawn."
The kid says to me:
"How much?"
I say nothing.
And she laughs.
I say she should mow the lawn because she lives in the house the lawn surrounds.
This makes her eyes roll up so hard that she almost loses consciousness.
I point out that we need to improve our productivity if we are going to keep up.
She wants to know who we are trying to keep up with.
I say the Joneses.
She grasps this concept immediately, being in junior high and a member of The Abercrombie aristocracy and all.
We negotiate.
I offer $5.
She wants $20
I go to $7.50.
She counters at $15.
I start telling about when I was a kid, and she immediately agrees to the $7.50.
I assume we have an agreement.
We don't.
She has issues:
About her hair.
About sweating.
About her friends seeing her.
I say mow at night.
She asks about a late-shift differential.
We continue to bargain.
She wants to know about fringe benefits.
I point out she already receives food, clothing, shelter, full medical, 24-hour maid and chauffeur service, and a weekly allowance.
She wants a 401(k).
Oh:
And she wants assurances none of the lawn-care work will be out-sourced.
Out-sourced?
You know, she says, like hiring the dweeb down the street to do the trimming, or buying a mulching mower that would eliminate the need for raking.
This becomes a sticking point.
The discussions get heated.
I call for a 30-day cooling-off period.

She is not, she says icily, "comfortable" with that.

I threaten to cut off her allowance.

She threatens a homework slowdown.

I suggest we seek the services of an in-house arbitrator.

She says her mother has a documented record as a proven management lackey.

Talks break off.

There is pressure on both sides.

She is forced to forego a back-to-school sale.

Neighbors are circulating petitions about the condition of the front lawn.

Talks resume.

There is movement.

She agrees to stop calling up the Teamsters Web site.

I promise to never hire the dweeb down the street.

As a show of good faith, she promises to stop debating, challenging, and arguing about every, single, little thing.

This makes my eyes roll up so hard that I almost lose consciousness.

Being Cold To Be Cool

It is early morning, cloudy and cool, and the kids on the corner waiting for the school bus are freezing.

You can tell this because there is no conversation and even less movement. They seem to be frozen in place and time.

Cold kids waiting for a bus are to be expected this time of year, but what makes this gaggle of teeth chatterers stand out is that their discomfort is self-inflicted.

The boys are wearing shorts and T-shirts, the girls light tops that barely reach their low-slung jeans.

There is not a coat or a sweater to be seen, even though the temperature is in the mid 40s. I don't get it.

I don't understand why anyone would choose to be cold. (I had an ex-girlfriend explain it to me once, but it was in a different context.)

One theory is that the shivering teens don't realize they are cold. They are aware that something seems to be causing them pain, but they can't quite put their finger it.

There are a lot of reasons given for this disconnect – unbridled hormones, hibernation patterns, living in a parallel universe – but the most plausible explanation may be that it is simply morning.

For those who have never owned a teenager, it is important to understand that until about noon, they have, on average, the brain-wave activity of a spoon.

Seriously, you can turn a fire hose on them for the first hour they're up, and they won't even grunt. So, you know, what's a little hypothermia?

It should also come as no surprise that teens are not on top of their game learning-wise in the a.m. Thus, it is unlikely that one morning's experiences are going to carry over to the next. Once frostbitten, twice shy? Not a chance.

Parents sometimes come under criticism for being indifferent to their teens' inadequate attire. I think this accusation is unfair, particularly when it comes to boys. I mean, who do you think stops them from leaving the house without their pants?

Aside from obliviousness, the other reason I think teens don't dress for the cold is because it's cool not to.

It's kind of an in-thing, like being psychotically grumpy or piercing what would otherwise be a perfectly good face.

In an effort to help untold numbers of young scholars avoid a premature cryogenic experience, we need to create some type of early warning system. One option might be an index – The Teen-Chill Factor? – which could be included in weather forecasts.

I'm not exactly sure how this works, but the formula could include such variables as temperature range, clothing choices, outdoor waiting time and the estimated amount of functioning brain matter available between 6 and 8 a.m.

The goal, of course, would be to drive by bus stops in January and see all the teens wearing hats, gloves and big warm coats – with their shorts.

Go Forth And Seize The *Zzzzzzzzs*

To this year's graduating class:

I stand before you today not to talk about your bright and shining future, which is apparently limitless; or to stress the importance of setting goals, like finding a cure for cancer or getting out of your parents' basement; or to wax philosophical about every ending being a new beginning, which has always seemed like a vicious circle to me.

No, the advice I offer you today as you take the path of endless possibilities that leads to the real world is this:

LEARN TO SLEEP LIKE AN ADULT.

For the past four years, you have slept like a college student. You have studied hard; you have partied hardy. And then you have collapsed into a comatose state over the weekend for 12 or 14 straight hours.

Although you may not be aware of this, most businesses do not operate on a college timetable. This means your start time will not be 9 a.m. one day, 1 p.m. the next, with Fridays as a free day. Rather, it is very likely you will be required to show up every day at the ungodly hour of 8 or 9 a.m.

Not only that, but when you arrive at work, you will be expected to be in a state closely approximating consciousness. This means brain-wave activity, blinking and acknowledging the presence of other life forms.

Here is another harsh reality:

If, say, you have an 8 a.m. meeting, you are probably not going to be able to blow it off and then get the notes from someone. Rare is the business that has a cuts policy. What businesses do have, however, is a policy in which you are handed an empty box and then escorted to your car by security guards.

Now, as alarming as this may seem, the post-college world is not as bad as it sounds if you do one thing – get enough sleep.

So how do you do that?

Did you ever notice those people you pass on their way to bed as you are on your way out for the night? You know who I mean: your parents, the folks you often see reading the newspaper in the morning when you are on your way in. Well, they are excellent adult-sleep role models.

What they have mastered over the years is something called a workweek sleep pattern. In simple terms, a workweek sleep pattern involves going to bed at the same time and getting up at the same time. If you do this on a consistent basis, you will develop something called energy. Energy is a major key – along with sucking up – to success in the real world.

And so, graduates as you go forth to pursue all your tomorrows, today, remember to dream, to dream big, to dream often.

Just don't hit the snooze button.

CHAPTER 6

LIFE AS WE KNOW IT

We take the weirdness – 5 stages of car repair? – for granted

How I Really Spent My Vacation

I am throwing my support behind Truth in Vacationing.

I am taking this stand because I believe the credibility of vacation recounting has reached an all-time low.

In workplaces all across America during summer, the following conversation takes place at a rate that can only be described as alarming:

"So, how was your vacation?"

"Terrific, great, fantastic, but just way too short."

Before exploring the question of why, in the history of modern vacationing, no one has ever come back to work and said they had a lousy time, let's take a quick look at the above-cited vacationers' actual experience:

The destination: A small, funky-smelling clapboard-covered oven, within walking distance of the beach (if you are a Navy Seal), for which he has agreed to pay $2,000 a week up front, sight unseen.

The packing: The initial loading of the family SUV took only four hours, but then everything had to be unloaded and repacked after it was realized that buried somewhere among the cargo were the car's only set of keys, the directions and the dog.

The trip: Because of space limitations, here are the highlights: the traffic jam, the overheating, the tow, the whining, the barking, the shouting, the silent treatment, the regurgitation, the wrong turn, the dog's accident, the driver's accident, the ticket, the naughty words, the handcuffs.

The beach: The beach was small, except when the tide was out, at which point it transformed itself into a vast, unrelenting stretch of desert from which the ocean was not visible. The good news was that one could get used to the smell.

The sunburn: Exhausted from the trip, our vacationer and his family fell asleep in the sun and awakened only when the volunteer fire department began to wet them down as a precaution. The family was thereafter discouraged from using the beach for the rest of their stay by both the trauma-room doctors and the local fire marshal.

The cost (including but not limited to):

Seafood lunch eaten at a picnic table on the edge of a busy highway, $57.

Purchase of matching T-shirts that say "I'm With Stupid," $49.

Round of miniature golf, $60.

Admission to water-slide park, $100.

Dinner eaten on outdoor terrace overlooking swamp marsh, $130.

Having a 16-year-old sales clerk take out scissors and cut up the Visa, priceless.

As for why no one in the history of modern vacationing has ever come back to work and admitted to having a lousy time, I have no idea. This is because all of my vacations have always been:

"Terrific, great, fantastic, but just way too short."

Learning The Webbed-Foot Wobble And Feeling Just Ducky

If ever there was a time to get out of the wet and into a dry martini, it is during one of our New England rainy spells.

When you look out the window and see the animals lining up by twos, you know it's time to start checking eBay for lifeboats.

Not that I'm anti-rain.

I love rainy days and rainy nights, and there is only one thing I enjoy more than taking a nap on a rainy afternoon, which, of course, is taking a nap at work. But then getting paid to sleep has always been my dream job.

Rain makes people behave strangely.

At the first drop, some people put on enough protective gear to handle enriched uranium. I blame mothers for this. Mothers do everything but Saran-Wrap their kids before sending them out in the rain. Kids never get over this. For every adult with a rubber fetish, there is a pair of galoshes lurking in his or her childhood.

Another weird group the rain brings out is the umbrella people. The umbrella is a fairly effective rain deterrent, in theory. In the hands of too many people, however, it is an instrument of mayhem and amusement, particularly when it malfunctions. Real men, by the way, do not use umbrellas.

Then there are the rain romantics, the crazy couple holding hands and skipping through the puddles, soaked to the bone. Interestingly, you never see any of these couples doing their duck dance a second time. This is because most of them die of pneumonia. They should have listened to their mothers.

Finally, there are the ditherings, a subset of which I am a member. Our dilemma is this: When caught in a downpour, we can't decide whether we will get less wet by running or walking through the rain drops. Personally, I run hunched over waving my arms back and forth in front of my legs.

While rain tends to make pedestrians move faster, it slows traffic to a crawl. I may have mentioned this before, but the reason for this is the rain people.

In brief, the rain people are a squad of nervous nellies who sit around a ready room in leather jackets and white silk scarves playing cards. When it starts to rain, a siren sounds and a voice screams "scramble, scramble" and they sprint to their idling vehicles and take off for the highway.

Once they get on the highway, the rain people zip along until they get in front of me. At this point they begin driving at a funeral-procession pace with both hands on the wheel, at least two feet on the brake, and their noses pressed against the fogged-over windshield.

Makes you wonder why wet people stop at one martini.

A Town Called Passing Gas (Really)

Allow me to suggest "Passing Gas."

It will give you a warm feeling.

It will make you smile.

And it can serve as a most entertaining diversion on, say, a long airplane flight.

"Passing Gas And Other Towns Along the American Highway" is a great book by photographer Gary Gladstone, who traveled to 60 U.S. towns with strange names and shot portraits that captured the essence of each locale.

Gas, by the way, is in Kansas, and folks who live there like to tell visitors not to blink or you'll pass Gas.

Maybe you have to be there.

One of the things the book will get you thinking about is why people who live in towns called Nuttsville (Virginia) or Odd (West Virginia) or Goofy Ridge (Illinois) don't do something about the name.

You'd think that after the third or fourth time you had to tell someone you come from Suck-Egg Hollow (Tennessee), you'd be calling for a town council vote – or Allied Van Lines.

Which is not to disparage Suck-Egg Hollow, which is probably a fine place, or those who live there, who I'm sure are fine people.

But, I mean, you have to think life is tough enough without, you know, going through it as a Suck-Egg Hollow-ite.

Then again, maybe it's an advantage in a boy-named-Sue kind of way to hail from Pig (Kentucky) or Tightwad (Missouri) or Stinking Point (Virginia), which you may be relieved to know is not in the immediate vicinity of Gas.

Anyhow, to personalize "Passing Gas," I have grouped towns mentioned in the book into categories:

Towns I would not admit being from:
Suckerville (Maine).
Crapo (Maryland).
Flushing (New York).
Toad Suck (Arkansas).
Towns I wouldn't mind being from:
Sweetlips (Tennessee).
Knockemstiff (Ohio).
Zip City (Alabama).
Monkey's Eyebrow (Kentucky).
Towns I would like to visit:
Hell (Michigan).
Greasy Corner (Arkansas).
Yum Yum (Tennessee).
Intercourse (Alabama).

Towns that put a lot of pressure on your behavior:
Nice (California).
Delightful (Ohio).
Difficult (Tennessee).
Boring (Oregon).
Towns where I probably have relatives:
Mars (Pennsylvania).
Screamer (Alabama).
Looneyville (West Virginia).
Fleatown (Ohio).
Embarrass (Illinois).
Ding Dong (Texas).

Town I don't believe can possibly exist, and if it does exist I would only visit disguised as a handkerchief:
Boogertown, N.C.

In Touch With Your Inner Mechanic

The five stages of car repair:

Denial

Is something wrong with the car? That noise is getting louder and louder. When I put on the brakes, should exhaust come out of the overhead light? Am I imagining all this? Maybe I'm just blowing this all out of proportion. Maybe it's just temporary. Hey, maybe I'm dreaming. Yo, wake up. OK, I'm awake, and it's still making the noise. You know, maybe it's supposed to make that noise. I'll bet all new cars make a noise that sounds like a drunken cat singing karaoke. I know, I'll turn up the radio and not think about it. There, that's better. Whew! I was really worried there for a while.

Anger

There is something wrong with my car. Why me? Of all the cars in the world, why do I get the one with the problem? There are lots of people out there who deserve to have car trouble more than me. Just my luck. And you know what else? Nobody cares. Look at all the other drivers out here on the road. They're just zipping by, not a care in the world, enjoying the day. Are they the least little bit concerned about my situation? No one gives a hoot that I may have a serious car problem. I hate my car. I hate the guy who sold me the car. But most of all I hate you.

Bargaining

All right, God, here's the deal. You give me a pass here, make the noise go away, and I swear I will be a changed man. I will be a force for good in the automotive world. I will crusade for changing the oil every 3,000 miles, for rotating the tires at regular intervals, for going to the car wash every week. Just let the mechanic tell me: "We found the noise, sir, it was a drunk cat singing karaoke. We pulled him out and gave him coffee. You're all set. No charge." So what do you say, God? Do we have a deal?

Depression

What's the point? Even if the noise did go away, there would just be another noise. There is always going to be a noise. I'm just one of those people who is always going to have a car that is always going to make a noise that is always going to lead to trouble. That's just the way it goes in this stinking world. Maybe I should just drive into a tree and put this car out of its misery. No one would even notice.

Acceptance

I'm going to have to bring the car into the dealer. I'm going to have to sit in the waiting room and watch daytime television. I'm going to have to pay through the nose. Then, on the way home, the car's going to make the same noise. Then I'm going to have to bring it back in. Then I'm going to have to sit in the waiting room and watch daytime television. Then I'm going to have to pay through the nose. Then, on the way home, the car's going to make the same noise. Then …

Leaders Give Democracy Bad Name

Q: How do you tell if a lawyer is lying?

A: His lips are moving.

A 70-year-old man jailed for telling that joke at a Long Island courthouse eventually had his case dismissed by a grand jury. He had been arrested for disorderly conduct, after a lawyer who heard the joke complained. One can only imagine what charges the guy might have faced if the joke had actually been funny:

Q: What do you call 20 lawyers skydiving from an airplane?

A: Skeet.

Or

Q: What do lawyers use for birth control?

A: Their personalities.

Although I have only anecdotal evidence to support this assertion, I believe power is corrupting the powerful at an increasingly amusing rate.

Why else wouldn't a judge have immediately thrown out this case?

Actually, I know why:

Q: What do you call a lawyer with a 50 IQ?

A: Your honor.

Meanwhile, the Virginia House of Delegates just passed a bill that will impose a $50 fine for anyone who displays his or her underpants in a "lewd or indecent manner."

The legislation is aimed primarily at young people who wear their pants so low that they drag around their under drawers.

While the Virginia legislature was no doubt sincere in efforts to quell this "Boxers Rebellion," they have in their haste crafted a law rife with loopholes.

Suppose, for example, young people opt to skirt the measure by not wearing any underwear at all, thereby exposing an unsuspecting citizenry to the horror of random encounters with peek-a-boo cheek cleavage?

Or suppose young people take to wearing their underpants over their regular pants, a fashion statement that would make their regular pants their underpants? And, if this bill were to become law, has anyone given any thought whatsoever as to where you are going to get a plumber?

While there is no question the elected officials in Virginia favor a baggy-pants approach to governing, they are veritable deep thinkers when compared to the Oklahoma legislature.

There, to get around a ban on cockfighting, a state senator has proposed that the roosters be allowed back in the ring as long as they are wearing tiny little boxing gloves on their feet.

In addition, he wants them to sport lightweight vests, which would be wired to record hits and keep score.

And, hey, if that doesn't work out, maybe they could outfit the feisty birds in old clothes and goggles and have them fight duels with paint-ball guns.

Yeah, power amuses, and absolute power amuses absolutely.

Why People Are Rude

I've been reading this report about how rudeness is getting worse in America.

You want to know why rudeness is getting worse?

People are jerks. If people didn't act like jerks, then people like you and me wouldn't have to be rude to them.

The report says that one of the places where rudeness is especially prevalent is on the highway.

You want to know why there is so much rudeness on the highway?

Because everybody else out there is a moron.

If everyone else out there wasn't a moron, then people like you and me wouldn't have to drive so aggressively to keep them from passing us.

I don't know, I guess I'm always a little suspicious of these types of surveys.

Take, for example, the matter of foul language.

On the one hand, 56 percent of respondents said they were "bothered a lot" when they heard someone curse, but 36 percent said they cursed up a storm themselves.

I mean, $%#@&**, this is why these kinds of &%$**!! reports are usually %$&**!#.

Having said that, one area where I think the report is right on has to do with cellphone usage.

Nearly half the people surveyed said they are often subjected to loud and annoying cellphone conversations.

You want to know why people are subjected to loud and annoying cellphone conversations? Because too few of us go over and rip the cellphone out of the obnoxious yakker's hand and throw it into the nearest body of water.

If more of us did this, then fewer of them would be inclined to treat their iPhones as a dinner partner.

But then, would such behavior on our part be considered rude?

Or do two rudes make a right?

The report is also accurate when it comes to rudeness and sales people.

According to the survey, 77 percent of respondents said it is common for sales people to "act like the customer is not even there."

You want to know why sales people act like the customer is not even there?

Because they have neurological problems.

And you know why they have neurological problems?

Because the multitude of decorative studs they have stuck in their heads have caused them to be repeatedly struck by lightning.

(OK, so I made that up.)

Know what drew the most negative response in the entire survey – computerized telephone answering systems.

A whopping 94 percent said they get really angry and frustrated when they call a business and are greeted by a recording.

You want to know why callers go so ballistic over such a reception?

Press this.

Thoughts About Heavy Thankers

We are heavy thankers.

By this I don't mean we do a lot of thinking.

It's important to make this distinction, because in my old neighborhood, thank was often the present tense of thunk, which was the past tense of think.

So if somebody said someone was a heavy thanker, it could mean he had thunk up a lot of important stuff.

Although this sounds a little confusing, it really wasn't.

You could always tell a heavy thanker because he would walk around scratching his head – even if it didn't itch.

When I say we are heavy thankers, I of course mean we spend a great deal of time engaged in thanking.

In fact, there are now almost no aspects of human interaction to which we are granted immunity from an exchange of thanks and yous.

Thank about it:

We thank to be polite – Thank you.

We thank to be indignant – THANK YOU.

We thank out of anger – Thanks for nothing.

We thank to refuse – Thanks, but no thanks.

We thank to accuse – Thanks to you.

We thank to praise – Thanks to me.

We thank out of pity – And that's the thanks I get?

We thank to single out – Special thanks.

We thank without skill – Thanks awfully.

We thank because we are thanked – I should be thanking you.

We thank to out thank – Thanks again.

We thank the masses – Thanks to all the little people.

We thank the universe – Thank your lucky stars.

We thank the heavens – There apparently being more than one.

We thank the past – Thanks for the memories.

We thank the calendar – Thank God It's Friday.

We thank to get in the last thank – No, thank you. No, thank you. No, thank YOU.

As if all this thanking is not enough, we also thank in multiples of thanks, as in:

Many thanks.

Much thanks.

Thanks a million.

Thanks a bunch.

Thanks a bundle.

And the ultimate thank in terms of sheer volume – Thanks loads.

As a result of this run of mindless thanking, the thank you has lost all meaning, for which, it should be noted, we have only ourselves to thank – thank you.

What to do?

Obviously, we cannot, as a culture, continue to thank at this pace. But if we ban the thank-you, how do we then express genuine feelings of gratitude and appreciation?

I'm stumped.

Maybe I'll ask one of the old neighborhood's heavy thankers if this is something he has ever thunk about.

Keeping Little Johnny From Seeing Red

I just read where more and more teachers are using less and less red ink on students' papers.

Seems red ink is too "aggressive," and too "frightening" and makes the little scholars feel bad.

The new color of failure is purple – like Barney.

Where were all these sensitive teachers when I was in school?

As I recall, my test papers usually came back looking like slasher-movie drop cloths.

There would be all these big red Xs and circled stuff, along with lots of multiple exclamation points and question marks.

And then, of course, there were the wholly unnecessary comments like:

"Did you even open the book????"

Or:

"You're a dope!!!!!"

This was particularly true when it came to anything involving math. My corrected math papers were so fiery bright, you had to wear a welder's helmet to look at them or risk permanent eye damage.

Here's what was, and continues to be, my major problem with math – it's too picky. You're either entirely right, or you're all wrong. There's no middle ground. And me, I'm a round-it-off, in-the-ballpark kind of guy.

Here is how I think all math problems should be graded:

Question: $1 + 1 = ?$

Answer: About 2.

The reason "color psychologists" say a purple marking pen is preferable to a red one is because the bluish element is less negative and more encouraging.

I don't know about that.

Personally, I don't see where it makes much difference what color an F comes in.

I mean, if the goal is to spare a failing student's feelings, why not just give him an A? I know that would work for me.

The reason teachers have always used red is because it is a color that tends to get one's attention.

Being graded in red is a lot like getting yelled at:

"It's here, not hair, you numbskull!!!!"

Purple, on the other hand, is like being counseled:

"If you could use here, not hair, in the future dear, you'll feel much better about yourself."

Now, which interaction is little Johnny apt to remember the next time the word choice comes up?

Another problem I have with purple is that grading in it makes even the brightest student's test paper appear dark and brooding.

And let's face it, people who spend a lot of time studying for tests are already depressed enough (or at least that's what I've always told myself).

I don't know, despite what the color psychologists say, I don't think the widespread use of red ink has ever done anyone any permanent damage.

I'm not sure you can say the same thing about Barney.

Spot, By Any Other Name, Still Smells

Naming a dog used to be simple.

You either gave your dog a traditional name – Fido, Rover, Old Blue – or an appearance-based name – Spot, Rusty, Socks – or a name derived from behavior – Digger, Bones, Nippy (or, in my experience, Howl, Chew and Pee).

Nowadays, because dogs are viewed as members of the family, the trend is toward giving them human names.

According to various websites, among the most popular dog names are Max, Jake, Buddy, Casey, Cody, Maggie, Molly, Lady, Lucy and Sandy.

When it comes to dog naming, no one takes it more seriously than owners of purebreds, who tag their pampered hounds with such appellations as Walsing Winning Trick of Edgerstoune, and Whisperwind on a Carousel, and Darbydales All Rise Pouchcove.

While these type names sound pretty fancy, they would never cut it in the real world. I mean, can you imagine yelling: "Here Walsing Winning Trick of Edgerstoune," or "Darbydales All Rise Pouchcove, sit."

The other thing to remember about aristocratic dog names is that they are still attached to animals who lick themselves in all the wrong places, enjoy sticking their noses into the business ends of other dogs and don't always get their drinking water out of their water bowl, if you catch my drift.

Men, of course, prefer to give dogs tough-guy names like Spike or Rocky or Killer, which, while sounding intimidating, do lose a bit of their edge when attached to, say, a Pekingese.

Which brings us to another thing men try to do – macho-up their mutt's breed:

"So, what kind of a dog you got there, pal?"

"This here is a French fighting dog, a Pit Poodle."

"What about your dog?"

"Attack, Bichon Frise."

Women, on the other hand, go in the opposite direction, emasculating muscular dogs like Shepherds and Dobermans by saddling them with names like Crocus and Piggy Wiggy.

And if you don't think dogs blush, you have never been introduced to a Great Dane called Pookie.

After spending more time than is probably necessary or normal, I have decided upon the name I want for my next dog. It was a tough choice, such possibilities as Mafioso, Xena, Burp, Brewskie, Uranus and Bob being eliminated along the way.

And the winner is – Stella.

And the reason is – I want to be able to go out on the back porch and, in my best Stanley Kowalski voice, scream, "STELLA. STELLA."

Creeped Out By Happy Campers

I'm thumbing through the new L.L. Bean summer catalog – and smiling.

I'm smiling because everyone in the catalog is smiling. Seriously, you cannot find one person in the entire booklet who is not smiling or smirking or working up one of the above.

Not only are the prominent people in the photos smiling, but so are the backup people as well as the people who aren't even supposed to be in the shot.

If that's not enough, on one page there are two puppies sleeping, and one of them is smiling. On another page, a fisherman is holding a large trout, which – and I used a magnifying glass to verify this – is smiling. And I'm not just talking grin here, I'm talking a humungous Julia Roberts smile.

All the smiling gets kind of creepy.

This is particularly true of the women's section, which could easily be titled "The Stepford Wives Try Out New Clothes."

You have to wonder how these people are able to smile so much and for so long. Are they professional smilers? Do they have trained teeth? Does it help to be demented?

Certainly, one explanation for the smile-a-thon is that L.L. Bean wants its models to convey the impression that they are happy to be promoting the company's products.

This feel-good-about-it philosophy seems to be pretty much standard industrywide, the major exception being the full-page fashion models seen in The Sunday New York Times, who are never smiling.

The Times' female models usually look either sultry or bored or preoccupied, while at the same time sending the unmistakable message that: I'm gorgeous, way out of your league – why does this sound familiar? – and if you dare approach me, I'll pepper-spray you to within an inch of your miserable little life.

In comparison, The Times' male models don't convey anywhere near the complexity. In fact, judging by their expressions, you'd have to say they are probably thinking: Maybe I should have shaved. Or: Wonder if she carries pepper-spray?

Another thing about the people in the L.L. Bean catalog is that none of them – with the exception of a couple of women and the trout – is ever making eye contact with you, the reader. They're either looking at each other or looking at someone or something amusing off-camera.

I can't imagine what. I've been to Maine, and it's just not that funny a place.

The people are OK, when you get to know them, but a fairly common first impression when you visit there is that you just walked into the middle of the annual constipation festival.

You know, given that we're talking about Maine here, maybe there is a very simple explanation for all the catalog's happy faces – the smiles are frozen in place.

CHAPTER 7

BABY BOOMERS

Will you still need us, will you still heed us, when we're 64?

Boomers Rule

It's always been about us.

And why not?

We had the numbers.

We had the chutzpah.

We had Wavy Gravy, who once said:

"If you can remember Woodstock, you probably weren't there."

Yeah, we were cool, all right.

Now, though, we're "Reelin' in the Years."

Time isn't just no longer on our side. Time is changing sides.

Other generations might see this getting-older thing as a problem.

We see it as a minor adjustment, such as reading glasses, Lipitor and forgetting stuff – like your spouse at the store.

Big freakin' deal.

So what if our flashbacks have gone the way of our hot flashes: 60 is the new 40; 40 is the new 20; 20 is the new, what? "Terrible Twos?"

All baby boomers, of course, are not created equal.

While baby boomers are broadly identified as those born between 1946 and 1964, the demographic is often divided into two groups.

You have your "Leading-edge" boomers (1946-55).

You have your "Trailing-edge" boomers" (1955-64).

Trailing-edge boomers are just entering the Fabulous 50s and trying to figure out how to send the kids to college and save for their golden, make that graying, years. (Hint: Either be really rich, Powerball lucky, or plan on working into your 70s.)

Leading-edge boomers began turning 62 this year and are starting to think about – retirement is definitely the wrong word here – what to do next.

For the first time in a long time, the nest is empty. They not only have freedom but also the time to spend it. So what's it going to be?

Kick back in a rocking chair – oh, please!

Run (or power-walk) with the bulls – maybe.

Write the great American novel – an option.

Change the world – been there, done that.

Learn to program your cellphone – anything's possible.

Trip the light fandango, turn cartwheels across the floor.

Bingo.

Older Drivers

Should older drivers be required to have their driving skills tested on a regular basis?

This is going to become a bigger and bigger issue as baby boomers (and their parents) move en masse into the land of the perpetual turn signal.

My thinking is:

Should middle-aged morons be required to have their driving skills tested on a regular basis after they have done something particularly stupid?

Should teenagers be required to have their driving skills tested on a regular basis based on the way they actually drive (talking on a cell phone and/or text messaging)?

Hey, studies have shown that operating a vehicle and talking on a cell phone simultaneously is the equivalent of driving drunk. As for text messaging while behind the wheel, people in the throes of a grand mal seizure are more alert.

Back to older drivers.

Let's face it, some people are capable of driving well into older age, and some aren't. Some people will recognize that they shouldn't be driving anymore, and some won't give up the car until someone pries the steering wheel from their cold, dead fingers.

The key is figuring out when to turn in the keys. One indicator may be how funny you find the following joke:

I want to die in my sleep like my grandfather, not yelling and screaming like the other people in his car.

Seriously, what we need is a standardized set of guidelines that everyone can use for self-evaluation.

Rock & Roll, Or Rocker?

The Rolling Stones were coming to a stadium near me.

One part of my brain was going, like: The Rolling Stones, man.

The World's Greatest Rock 'n' Roll Band, man.

Gotta see the Stones, man. Gotta.

The other part of my brain was less psyched. Sounding distressingly like Ward Cleaver, it was wondering:

Will there be adequate security?

Will the music be too loud?

Will you be too tired for work the next day?

Who will baby-sit for the Beaver?

Back when Mick was a prime-time tour de prance, and Keith Richards still had the look of a viable life form, there would have been only one voice. It would have shouted:

Dip into your college fund.

Sleep outside the ticket window.

Seize the Stones.

But a quarter-century-or-so later, I found myself caught between hard rock and a soft place – middle age.

What to do?

I made lists, a pathetic gesture in and of itself.

The advantages were obvious:

"(I Can't Get No) Satisfaction." "Let's Spend the Night Together." "Start Me Up." "Jumpin' Jack Flash."

The concerns, unfortunately, came just as quickly:

Do the stadium seats provide lumbar support?

Are the restrooms close by?

Will I have to stand for the entire show?

Are relaxed-fit jeans uncool?

What if I smell something illegal?

What if my wife wants to sit on my shoulders?

Essentially, it came down to this:

I was eyeball-to-eyeball with Mick Jagger, staring directly into the bloodshot windows of his lost soul, and all I was seeing was my own reflection.

It made me blink.

I told everyone I didn't go to the concert because it was too cold. But if the weather had not provided me with a convenient excuse, I would have found something else. I would have developed car trouble or a schedule conflict or some other sober, reasoned, responsible cop-out.

No, it isn't easy coming to terms with the realization that your kids now have a momma that don't dance and a daddy who don't rock 'n' roll.

It is even more difficult to face that you are in grave danger of becoming something you thought you could never, ever be: a fogy.

But, hey, Shinola happens. So you move on. You rationalize.

Seeing the Stones at this point would have been like going to one of those old-timer games where ballplayers with big guts limp around on creaky joints and everyone claps for yesterday.

Or maybe you tell yourself the last thing the world needs is another rhythm-impoverished boomer dancing the white-guy overbite and wondering why everyone else is out of step.

One thing you know for sure, though, is this:

You can't always get what you want.

And. . .

Time, in the long run, ain't on your side.

No Elder Speak, Dude

I've never been a big fan of baby talk.

You know the way some people get all high pitched and cooch-e-cooie when they come face to face with an infant who, being still months away from walking, is unable to flee.

Elderspeak is similar to baby talk.

The term may be new, but we're all familiar with the practice of referring to older people in such condescending terms as sweetie, pops, dearie and old-timer.

Although elderspeak is annoying and obnoxious, when you think about it, we spend our lives being addressed in bothersome ways.

When you are a kid, they call you kid.

"Hey, kid, can't you read? Get off the lawn."

When you get into your teens and 20s, people stop calling you kid and instead call you by your last name.

"Hey, Dingledorf, I've been telling you this for 20 years now. Get off the lawn."

In your 30s and 40s, people still call you by your last name, only now they are more apt to dress up the Dingledorf with a Mr., Miss, Mrs. or even a Ms.

"You are looking particularly uptight today, Ms. Dingledorf."

That said, when it comes to forms of address, nothing is more jolting than the first time one is called "sir" or "ma'am."

I think it is definitely worse to be called ma'am than sir, although I have never actually been called ma'am . . . OK, except for this one time by a football coach.

The reason I say ma'am is worse is because sir is more commonly used across a wide range of ages:

"Sir, I'll get that report to you in one hour," you say to the boss.

"May I see your license and registration, sir," the officer says to you.

Ma'am, on the other hand, connotes the crossing of some kind of matronly boundary.

One day you are Miss Dingledorf, and the next day the kid bagging your groceries is saying, "Can I put these in the car for you, ma'am?"

Baby boomers still have a way to go before becoming victims of elderspeak, but I'm already working on my response, which, allowing for various off-color modifiers, goes something like this:

Dude, kiss my ass.

Return Of "The One"

A word of warning to baby boomers.

If you have reproduced, and this past fall sent your progeny away to college, come Thanksgiving, your life will change.

On Thanksgiving Eve, laundry in tow, The One will return.

You will be happy, of course, to see them, and then you won't see them.

They will say "hi", "which car can I take", and "bye." Then they will be off to see their friends and won't be back home until well after you have gotten up the second time to go to the bathroom.

This will be one of the first adjustments you will have to make. And there will be many:

You will return to not being able to fall into a sound sleep until you hear the car pull into the garage in the early-morning hours.

You will be amazed at the large quantities of food gone missing from the refrigerator overnight.

You will feel guilty about making noise around the house before 1 p.m.

You will not find the washer and dryer empty at any time of the day or night.

You will consider calling the police to report strange people with bad facial hair lurking in the driveway before realizing they are The One's high school friends.

You will have running spats over minor matters, which are actually disputes over a bigger thing . . . independence.

If you have other children still at home, the return of The One will not be as jarring because the loss of privacy will not be as great.

But if it has just been the two of you, or the one of you, for the past three months, giving up the new lifestyle you are gradually embracing more and more will be surprisingly difficult.

After all, it has been hard-earned emotionally.

You have no doubt gone through the five stages of dropping your first, or last child, off at college:

Separation and a sense of loss.

Long-distance worrying.

Getting used to it.

Getting to like it.

Walking around the house naked.

The good news is that the inaugural return of The One will be over in a flash and within a few days you will have readjusted.

The bad news is that, in a matter of weeks, The One will be back, and this time it will be for a month.

Good luck with that.

From Rabbit Ears To High-Def

Television and baby boomers grew up together.

We were there when sets were the size of Buicks and screens the size of hubcaps.

The picture, when there was one, was in black and white, and the reception, when there was some, was similar to peering out a window into a blizzard.

High-tech houses had large antennas on their roofs. Low-tech houses had rabbit ears, which had to be positioned just right.

Sometimes this involved standing in a corner on one foot facing the wall while holding the rabbit ears in one hand and a large serving spoon in the other. (Being the youngest in the family had some major drawbacks.)

While televisions built in the last 30 years or so generally die slowly from obsolescence, the first sets had the life expectancy of an Edsel.

When the set didn't come on, or when it suddenly turned itself off, the usual culprit was a tube or tubes. If it was a minor tube, one could go to the local hardware store and plug it into a tester. If the problem was the picture tube, your set was pretty much totaled.

As for viewing, there were only three channels at first, and you knew what show was on what channel at what time because it was the same every week.

If you wanted to change the channel, it required getting up, walking over to the set and turning the knob. Once this was accomplished, it was often necessary to reposition the person standing on one foot in the corner holding the rabbit ears and serving spoon.

Because there was only one TV in the house, and everyone watched it together, changing the channel was not only a physical challenge but an interpersonal one as well. Votes were taken, coalitions formed, compromises made, dictatorial powers often employed.

These days we sit in front of 60-inch high-definition televisions clicking on everything, watching nothing. We are not so much interested in what is on as what else is on or what will be on.

Today, such shows as "I Love Lucy," "The Adventures of Ozzie and Harriet" (they had adventures?) and "The Honeymooners" wouldn't stand a chance. As for the Beaver, if he was found anywhere, it would be on "Animal Planet."

AARP Must Fall

There comes a point in every baby boomer's life when, without warning, he or she gets in the mail an unsolicited greeting from AARP.

It seems to me that this initial contact comes shortly after you turn 21, but others have assured me that it does not, in fact, come to pass until you have hit the big 5-oh.

Becoming AARP mailing-list eligible has become a rite of passage, albeit a sobering one. It is a cold slap in the face from the future. You see your life flash before you. It is wearing Depends.

After the initial shock, most new AARP recruits go through a long process that eventually leads to a place of contentment. But to get there, one must first experience the five stages of AARP:

DENIAL: This can't possibly be happening to me. There must a mistake. I'm too young. I have kids in high school. I'm cool. I'm awesome. I Facebook. I text. I Twitter. I wear jeans. I blast the radio and play air guitar. This can't be. No! No! No!

ANGER: I am not going to stand for this. This is insulting. This is no way to treat a middle-aged person. I am going to get a hold of these AARP people and let them have it. No, better yet, I'm going to call my lawyer. I'm going to sue them for mental cruelty, pain and suffering, and wanton negligent mistaken identity. Maybe I should send them a photo?

BARGAINING: All right, I'll tell you what. If AARP promises not to send me any more unsolicited materials, and not to contact me again until I am 65, I'll join the organization then and become a model member. I'll be the perfect senior. I'll wear sensible shoes. I'll grow bushy eyebrows. I'll drive a big car really slowly. I'll eat out at 5 p.m. I'll rail at the neighborhood children and scream, "You kids today have no respect."

DEPRESSION: What's the point? I'm old. Actually, now I'm officially old. My best years are behind me. My hair is turning gray. My crow's feet are developing crow's feet; my chins have chins. What do I have to look forward to – turning 60? I should die first in my sleep. Go away. I need a nap.

ACCEPTANCE: You know what, it's going to be OK. So what if AARP has me in their sights? No one is making me join. I'll just make believe the organization doesn't exist, although it does have some pretty good rates on insurance. If the day comes when I feel the need to join up, I will. It won't be the end of the world.

I mean, it's not like I'm moving to Florida.

Thanksgiving Comes With Side Of Reality

Thanksgiving has always been my favorite holiday.

It's totally hassle free.

You don't have to drag a tree into the house and get it to stand by itself. You don't have to feel guilty about not going to church. You don't have to go on a picnic on a 100-degree day and play horseshoes.

I would feel totally different about Thanksgiving, of course, if I was called upon to prepare the meal, which from afar does look like it takes some work.

Unfortunately, or fortunately, I don't cook. At all. OK, except for one dish, which really doesn't complement Thanksgiving dinner. That would be toast.

If you have a Thanksgiving Day craving for turkey, mashed potatoes and toast, I'm your guy.

This Thanksgiving, I had a most disturbing revelation.

As I sat among the turkey, stuffing, potatoes, gravy, pies and assorted fixin's, I realized that not only can I no longer eat as much, I didn't really mind stopping before nausea set in.

I don't think I'm alone in this. I've talked to other boomers who admit they are disinclined to pack it away the way they did in days of yore.

To be sure, there are still plenty of boomers who can turn a 25-pound turkey into a carcass without ever leaving the table. But for me, that gravy boat has sailed.

This is unsettling. It almost makes me feel un-American. Like I'm not doing my part. Like I'm letting down the Pilgrims or something.

Granted, there are advantages to not eating like a 350-pound nose tackle. For one thing, you aren't so full that you not only want to loosen your belt, you want to drop your pants. Nor are you asking people to dial 911 because you've lost the ability to burp.

Besides not being able to eat as much, I also noticed this Thanksgiving that I have suffered a decrease in the time I can remain conscious while watching the mandatory post-feast football game.

Can't eat as much. Can't stay awake to watch football. What's next? Remaining completely sober on New Year's Eve?

Mother of God, don't tell me that's in the cards.

Worse Than A Date:
Trying To Get A Date

I think dating is probably easier today than when baby boomers were in play.

Not that I have any first-hand knowledge. When you get married, there is this kind of an unspoken agreement that you won't date other people.

Most people are fine with the arrangement. In fact, one of the main reasons people get married is so they won't have to date anymore.

In the old days, dating as a social institution was at its most wrenching in high school. After this dark period, it got much easier. This is because a confidence-building component was added to the equation: beer.

The only thing worse than being on a date was getting the date. The process was excruciating, and this is if you were smooth. If you were like, well, the rest of us, even if you got the date, it was an exercise in humiliation.

For a date seeker, the phone call was the first option. Not that it was a great option, just that it was better than the second option, which was being rejected to your face, most likely in front of at least a dozen of her girlfriends (or so it seemed).

It was up to the boy to make the phone call. Girls didn't call boys for dates. Girls hung around and waited to be called. This created its own set of anxieties.

Imagine being a girl, and the phone rings, and without any warning or time for preparation you are forced to make a decision that will not only affect your Saturday night but the caller's sense of ego for the rest of his life.

The initial phone call didn't just happen. Before the number was dialed an approach had to be decided upon, courage summoned and an opening line memorized.

The last thing you wanted was to sound unsure, and/or for the girl to hear the sweat cascading off your forehead.

There were three general responses to a date call:

Best: An immediate yes.

Second-best: "I'm not sure. Tell me who you are again?"

Worst: Laughter.

Dating rules are less rigid these days, and modern communication tools such as e-mail, texting and instant messaging have relieved much of the pressure. If someone asks you for a date in writing, you have time to craft a response.

Even the old phone call is no longer as intimidating, thanks to voice mail and caller ID.

Of course, you still have to go out on the date, which is a whole other horror story.

Staggered Retirements Can Be Staggering

More and more baby-boomer couples are finding themselves in a situation where one is retired and the other is still slaving away.

The arrangement is fairly common. Fewer than one in five couples pack it in at the same time, according to AARP magazine.

But staggered retirements can cause (hostility is probably too strong a word) friction.

The basic problem is one of parallel universes. The retiree is in kick-back-and-relax heaven, while the working stiff remains in nose-to-the-grindstone hell.

Resentment often surfaces in the morning, when one half of the couple gets up for work, and the other just rolls over. This can make an otherwise considerate person do things like grind walnuts in the blender at 6 a.m.

To the working stiff, life still revolves around the work week: 9 to 5, Monday through Friday, 40 hours.

To the retiree, life takes on rounded edges. Days run together; the work week morphs into the 24/7 weekend. Monday is just Saturday with a fresh coat of paint.

After a while, moods begin to clash.

The stiff remains work-world wired, tense, stressed. This is particularly true at the end of the day, after the slings, arrows and extended fingers of the evening commute have been endured.

Meanwhile, the retiree is chilling, mellowing, but also becoming increasingly prone to crossing the thin line between cheerful and annoying.

It is not uncommon for the retired half to be so flush with euphoria that he or she fails to remember that if you have had just a wonderful, terrific, relaxing day, it's best to keep it to yourself.

Of course, there are cases in which the working half is happier than the non-working half. Personally, I have never known anyone in such a situation, but I guess anything is possible.

No, overall, I think retirement is kind of like eating garlic. Unless both parties are going to indulge, somebody's going to have a problem.

Ten Signs You May,
Or May Not, Be Losing It

10. You find yourself changing signal light bulbs once a week.

9. You are the focus of a neighborhood driving watch.

8. You are often followed by the emergency-personnel paparazzi.

7. You have relatives lining up to take out life insurance on you.

6. You recently got angry at someone who cut you off and gave them the thumb.

5. You own prescription night-vision goggles for driving after dark.

4. You are often tailgated by women pushing strollers.

3. You routinely take up three parking spaces at the mall.

2. You are thinking about replacing your Lincoln Town Car with something bigger.

1. You often pull into gas stations and sit there, waiting for the attendant to come out and fill the tank, check the oil and wash the windshield.

CHAPTER 8

THE OLD HOMESTEAD

Give the average guy a tool belt and he thinks he's Norm Abrams

Feeling The Heat On The Cold

It's October.

It's New England.

It's the time of the year when everyone is wondering the same thing.

When do you turn on the heat?

There are the physical indicators to consider:

Can you see your breath?

Is there a layer of frost on the rugs in the morning?

Have the plants turned black?

Has there been a confirmed case of frostbite?

When you invite guests for dinner, do they come in snowmobile suits?

Are any family members beginning to grow fur?

Right now, we are in "John Adams" mode in my house. By that I mean we are walking around nights draped in blankets like they did back in the 1700s.

When I say blanket, I don't mean big fluffy quilt or anything. I'm talking about more of a shawl, except I don't want to use the word shawl because I'm pretty sure one of the Real Men's Club bylaws specifically states: Real men don't wear shawls.

Of course, there was a time when we didn't worry about turning on the heat, a time when we wore T-shirts around the house in the dead of winter. But that was back before it was cheaper to burn dollar bills than oil.

You try wearing a T-shirt around the average house now in the dead of winter and you will be dead in winter.

The good thing about October is that while it can get nippy, the temperature fluctuations are still such that if your house gets too cold you have other options:

You can go outside to warm up.

You can use the fireplace, although with the price of wood these days it might be less expensive to burn the furniture . . . not that there aren't certain pieces of our furniture I wouldn't mind seeing going up in smoke.

You can go sit in the car and turn on the heated seats.

The bottom line is that deciding when to rouse the furnace is an individual decision based on personal circumstances:

How much cold can you stand?

What is your heating budget?

Is anyone in your house experiencing menopause? (Hot flashes can reduce a home's energy bills by as much as 75 percent.)

How comfortable are you wearing a shawl?

Jim From This Old House

When it comes to home repairs, I think I have above-average abilities. Others do not share this view.

I see myself as Tommy the carpenter from "Ask This Old House."

Others see me as "Tommy" from the rock opera of the same name.

I think that's a bit . . . harsh.

Have there been home-repair learning experiences along the way? Of course. Have there been occasions in which significant additional damage was done? Technically speaking, yes.

Have there been fires?

Absolutely not. Occasional wisps of smoke, the smell of melting rubber perhaps, but no visible flames.

That said, when I slap on the old tool belt these days, it is with a high degree of confidence.

There is only one thing I don't feel comfortable messing with around the house – the furnace. Furnaces are very temperamental. You turn one lousy little valve the wrong way, and trust me, you'd think Metro-North was pulling into your basement.

I also never used to fool with electricity, although I'm over that now. Not that I'm going to rewire the house or anything. But ever since I learned how to turn off the juice at the panel in the cellar, I can now do small jobs without worrying about touching the wrong wire and suffering a loss of bowel control.

This past weekend I replaced two lights and two faucets in the upstairs bathroom. The lights went in without a hitch. The faucets involved a lot of swearing. One of the first things you learn about plumbing is that swearing is much more important than expertise.

Before testing these new installations, I ran through the usual checklist, which, contrary to rumor, is not mandated by our homeowner's insurance carrier.

Did you alert the neighbors, fire department, police, hospital, Department of Homeland Security and clergy?

Check.

I was pleased with the way the job turned out.

When I hit the light switch, the hot water didn't come on.

And when I turned the faucet, the lights were not affected.

I really should have my own show.

Who Lives In The Living Room?

The living room is living a lie.

No one lives in the living room.

No one visits the living room.

Heck, I know people who have never even been in the living room.

With good reason.

What's the attraction? The decor is ugly, the ambience stiffer than a shot-and-beer joint, and you can't put your feet up on the furniture.

People who defend living rooms say they are necessary in case the minister or insurance man drops by unexpectedly.

I don't buy this.

First, if a minister ever approached my house there would be so much meteorological activity that there is zero chance his call would be a surprise.

Second, in recorded history, no briefcase-toting person wearing a sharp suit and a smile has ever rung my doorbell and found somebody home.

The living room is not the only space in the house that is mislabeled. The names assigned to every room in today's home are equally irrelevant.

This really needs to be fixed.

Dining Room: The name conjures up images of fancy plates, fine food, and eating with utensils. In reality, it is where you gather with in-laws two or three times a year.

Suggested name: The War Room.

Family Room: This is where everyone comes together every night to ignore each other while staring for hours on end at a flickering box.

Suggested name: Comatorium.

Bath Room: Is soaking in a steaming tub of one's own grime really the predominant activity that takes place here?

Suggested name: The Library.

Rec Room: Cheap paneling, old furniture, a ping pong table, and a television cannot hide the fact that this is still the cellar.

Suggested name: The Cellar.

Home Office: A desk, a computer, and a couple of boxes of paperclips do not an office make. Let's be honest.

Suggested name: The 1040 Forum.

Kitchen: Traditionally, this is the venue where stoves and ovens are located and stuff like baking and boiling takes place. Of course, no one cooks anymore.

Suggested names: The Nukeistry. The Thawery.

The Bedrooms: These room designations need to be broken down, because all bedrooms are not created equal.

Suggested names: Guest bedroom. Coat Room. Master Bedroom: Headache Place. Teen's Bedroom: The Landfill.

Finally, what to do with the living room.

Suggested name: Parlor, as in Billiards.

Tree Takes Out The Ho-Ho-Ho

In terms of grounds, I'm not saying it's up there with infidelity, mental cruelty or answering the "how-fat-does-this-make-me-look" question.

Nor do I mean to imply that as a factor it compares, say, to leaving underwear on the bedroom floor.

But there is no question that the major reason couples file for divorce this time of year is directly tied to one thing, and one thing only:

Putting up the Christmas tree.

Let's look in on Christmas Past and watch Tiny Jim and his family as they drag their $60 tree into the house.

As you can see, the base of the tree has been cut on an angle, which means it must be re-cut straight across so it will stand straight.

Here's Tiny Jim returning from the cellar with the family all-purpose handsaw.

Here is Tiny Jim sawing, sawing, sawing ... oops, the saw seems to be stuck. No matter how hard Tiny Jim tries, no matter how many veins in his forehead throb, he cannot move it.

Tiny Jim comes back from the cellar with the family 16-inch chainsaw. It makes noise, and blue smoke and chips, lots and lots of chips. Mrs. Tiny Jim does not look happy. Now Tiny Jim is holding the standard, four-legged, three-bolt Christmas tree stand.

In theory, the standard, four-legged, three-bolt Christmas tree stand is supposed to effortlessly attach to the bottom of the tree and then hold it straight and secure for the duration of the holidays.

In fact, the standard, four-legged, three-bolt Christmas tree stand does not do this because, in truth, the standard four-legged, three-bolt Christmas tree stand was invented by a moron.

There's Tiny Jim trying to slip the stand over the base of the tree. But no matter how hard he tries, it won't fit. There's Tiny Jim firing up the 16-inch chainsaw again.

Now the tree fits.

Tiny Jim is now crawling around on the floor trying to adjust the bolts that hold the tree. He is having problems, though, because there is sweat in his eyes, and sap has glued his hands to the stand.

Eventually, Tiny Jim gets all the bolts just right.

Mrs. Tiny Jim says the tree is leaning left. Tiny Jim adjusts some more.

Mrs. Tiny Jim says the tree is leaning right.

Finally, Mrs. Tiny Jim says the tree is perfect.

Tiny Jim gets up from the floor and stands back to admire his work.

The tree falls over.

There's Tiny Jim and Mrs. Tiny Jim on the phone.

They aren't calling Santa.

They are calling lawyers.

Painting Part I (Getting Started)

Drink sushi shakes.
Own a cat.
Date Ann Coulter.
Drive a minivan.
Vacation in Bosnia.
Iron.
Party with Orrin Hatch.
Perform my own vasectomy.
These are just a few of the things I would gladly do rather than paint.
Painting, and I'm talking about the application of color to wall here, is the most unsung and unappreciated of the fine arts.
Anyone can whip up a landscape, knock off a nude, or slap some traumatic aspect of their middle-class childhood onto a canvas in the name of abstraction.
But try to paint a white baseboard without getting anything on a blue rug.
Or how about doing a door without hitting the brass lock?
Or a textured ceiling.
Or – and just mentioning this gives my colon pause – window panes.
No, the ability to paint, to track a brush along an exposed edge while toying with only a millimeter margin of error, is more than just a skill. It is a talent, a gift, a genius to which you are born.
Or not.
When it comes to painting, I have been multiply cursed:
I have no talent or temperament for it.
I have no money to hire someone who does.
I have bare wood.
I have a spouse.
So . . .
I go to the paint store and the guy asks: oil or latex? I ask: What's the difference? And he says something about you can cover one with the other, but not the other with one. And I say what I always say when I don't understand a clerk's explanation: "Give me the cheapest."
I think about buying a paint brush, but then I remember we already have a paint brush, a big, wide one that covers wide spaces with each stroke.
I find the paint brush right where I left it, in the cellar in a Maxwell House coffee can half-filled with some kind of solvent.
I pull the brush from the can only to discover it is not only stiff, but attached to an inch-thick hunk of gunk.
I scrape the gunk off, but that leaves the end of the brush looking like it has just been electrocuted.
I grab a pair of pruning shears and give the frizzy bristles an old-fashioned buzz cut.
I open the cheapo paint with a screwdriver and start to stir, except I can't

because there is a kind of crust covering the top.

I remove the crust with a pair of borrowed eyebrow tweezers, which leaves a swirly, brownish-yellowish oil spill.

I mix the oil spill into the paint beneath, producing a solution that's runnier than a big nose in January.

Finally, I dip the buzz cut into the paint – the color of which is previously unfamiliar to mankind – and begin.

The screaming stops me in mid stroke.

Painting Part II (Getting Restarted)

We are back at the paint store.

We are here because the paint brush that had been soaking in the cellar in the solvent in the Maxwell House coffee could not be salvaged.

We are here because when we used the beat-up brush; it created a kind of wide-wale corduroy pattern on the wall.

Primarily, though, we are here because the owner of the eyebrow tweezers used to remove the layer of crust covering the original gallon of cheapo paint made threats of an anatomical nature.

This has resulted in a change of approach.

Ignorance is now being admitted. Questions are being asked. Advice is being taken. Visa is being deployed. Supplies are being purchased.

We walk out of the store with brushes, rollers, trays, thinners, edgers, tape and paint bearing the name of that renowned handyman Ralph Lauren.

The room is 12 by 12.

It has one door, one window, one ceiling, one floor, four walls, two light switches, three electrical outlets, moldings and a new rug.

The plan is to paint the trim a high-gloss white and everything else a bottom-of-a-municipal- swimming-pool blue.

The job will be difficult, delicate.

It will require nerve, a steady hand, arrogance.

It will be like brain surgery without all the beeping.

It will leave no room for oops.

Although we are now psychologically prepared to begin the laying on of latex, from a practical perspective, we are, in fact, still hours away.

As the late Green Bay Packers coach Vince Lombardi used to say about painting: "Preparation isn't everything, it's the only thing."

So we go down into the cellar and come back with a stack of old newspapers.

Additional trips yield rags, sandpaper, scrapers.

Additional trips yield ladders, buckets, lights.

Additional trips yield tape, tarps, tools.

We begin.

We stir, and stroke, and roll, and cut in, and wipe up, and sweat, and ache, and develop a Category V migraine from the designer fumes and the glare of the bare lightbulb. But we finish.

The inspection by the owner of the eyebrow tweezers used to remove the layer of crust covering the original gallon of cheapo paint goes as expected:

"You missed a spot here."

"You got paint on the rug there."

And then the clincher:

"It needs a second coat."

We stick the new brush in the old solvent in the Maxwell House coffee can – and just walk away.

Domestic Geese: Resident Evil

Sometimes I get up during the night and check no man's land from the window.

Sometimes I slip out the front and then quietly sneak through the woods to outflank them.

And sometimes I just fling open the back door and charge half-clothed into the yard screaming "Heeeeere's Johnny!"

Some people in my neighborhood think I'm disturbing the peace. Other people in my neighborhood think I'm just disturbed.

Geese will do that to you.

Geese will get under your skin and into your head until one day you're riding a kid's tricycle around the house mumbling "red rum, red rum, red rum."

Sure, every homeowner sooner or later does battle with wildlife. And I've fought my share of squirrels over the bird feeder, and mice over the kitchen cupboards, and moles over the lawn.

This is different, though.

This has turned into a fight for a way of life, for the right to walk barefoot in the backyard and not be afraid that a misstep will send a wet muck of greenish yuck oozing up through your toes.

Just to be clear, I have no problem with migrating geese. My beef is with the resident goose, a lazy, loud, messy freeloader who is really nothing more than a pigeon in a fat suit.

Experts say the most effective way to control the exploding goose population – exploding geese, now there's a concept – is through increased hunting.

Perhaps the time has come to turn the guys in the orange vests loose.

Perhaps the hour has arrived to focus the vast firepower possessed by private citizens.

Perhaps goose hunting should include the following seasons:

Automatic weapon season.

Hand grenade season.

Small aircraft strafing season.

Surface-to-goose missile season.

And for densely populated areas, what about handgun season?

Now, I realize there are people out there who favor a less belligerent approach. And before we go hard nose to tail feathers with the geese – most unsettling imagery – I am all for giving goose sympathizers a chance to work out a peaceful solution to the conflict.

I mean, if they want to:

Train the geese to use Port-O-Johns, fine.

Hold frank discussion about abstinence, fine.

Distribute tiny little condoms, fine.

Slap a pair of Depends on the entire population, fine.

But understand this ... oops, sorry, gotta go.

Heeeeere's Johnny!

The Rock Of Ages

Spring means outdoor projects.

Like the rock.

It looks to be the size of a football.

Mossy. Gray. Dull.

Stupid looking, too.

Certainly nothing you'd make a pet of.

And it has to go.

Not because it is in the way of anything but because you have stared out at it on the lawn all winter and, frankly, it has come to offend your sense of grooming.

So on a pleasant spring morning you grab a shovel and set out.

Day I

Shouldn't take long, you figure – a 10-minute job at most.

An hour of digging later, a perimeter has yet to be established.

If you are correct, the rock is not a rock but a boulder.

In terms of comparison, a rock is to a boulder what a breadbox is to a boxcar.

You go back to the garage for more tools.

Three hours, a pick, a pry bar, a sledge hammer, a broken shovel, a major blister and what may have been a mild heart episode later, you are about to quit. When it moves – you think.

You break for lunch.

You return with chains and ropes.

Men have gathered.

Nothing attracts the male neighbor like an open hole.

Questions are asked. Advice offered. Tools pledged.

No one mentions doing any digging.

You continue to excavate.

The hole is now legally deep enough to bury a coffin.

This, you are beginning to think, could come in handy.

Finally, chains are strung from boulder to rear bumper.

Horsepower is applied.

The boulder doesn't move.

The rear bumper does.

Night falls.

Day II

The backhoe man arrives.

He comes in a loud truck with a yellow machine in tow.

Men stream out of homes.

Heavy equipment is to the male neighbor what the ice cream truck is to kids.

The backhoe man walks slowly around the hole. Then he says:

"Nice hole."

This is like Mark McGwire saying nice swing.
Or Bill Gates saying nice computer.
Or Monica Lewinsky saying nice, well, anyway ...
The backhoe man goes to work.
The hole gets bigger.
The day grows longer.
The boulder doesn't move.
The backhoe man reaches several conclusions. In order they are:
"That ain't a boulder, it's the top of a mountain."
"You're wasting your time."
"That will be 400 bucks."
Night falls.
Rain falls.

Day III

The man from the blasting company shows up.
He walks slowly around the hole. Then he says:
"Nice pond."
You ask about explosives.
He says it will be a big job.
You ask how big.
He says mushroom cloud.
You ask the next logical question:
How big a mushroom cloud?

Wanted: Friendly Flamethrower

Anyone know where you can pick up a decent used flamethrower?

I've had it with snowblowers.

I'm sick of wrestling them.

I'm sick of having to stop every two seconds and clear them.

I'm sick of them spitting snow back into my face.

I'm telling you, if it weren't for the fact that snow shovels cause more heart attacks than bacon cheeseburgers, I'd go back to using one.

This despite the fear that if I did have a heart attack shoveling snow, it would probably occur just as I was done clearing the driveway.

And to make matters worse, the neighborhood kid/extortionist that I refused to hire to do the job would probably be standing there watching.

I can envision the conversation:

"Kid, call an ambulance."

"$20 bucks."

"I'll give you $10."

"$15. Cash."

"OK, you little ... ''

The last storm was the final straw. Who knew it could snow cement?

I was about halfway through when Kong, my snowblower, conked.

This was kind of disappointing because up until now, Kong had been, as advertised, a beast. It devoured snow in huge gulps, blew it thousands of feet into the air, and was fast enough to do airport runways.

In retrospect, buying it had been a bit of an overreaction to the limitations of my previous snowblower, The Wuss, which worked fine as long as it was tackling snow one flake at a time.

Anyway, I was not surprised when Kong broke down, because the one-year warranty had run out 10 days earlier, which meant the belly-up was right on schedule.

So I called the repair guy, who told me it was going to be two weeks before I would get Kong back, meaning I had to either pray it wouldn't snow or find another option.

I thought about getting someone to plow, but that arrangement never seems to work for me.

Although I don't want to disparage all snow plowers, the ones I have dealt with were always too eager to show up when there was a couple of inches on the ground, and nowhere to be found when there was a foot. (My theory is that when there is a foot of snow or more, snow plowers hang out at the same place home-improvement contractors do when the job is half finished.)

This is why I'm thinking flamethrower.

It will clear the snow without exertion and keep you warm at the same time. Plus, it can be used for other purposes, such as autumn leaves, and if that isn't enough to get the male heart wildly thumping, let me toss out one other possibility – grilling.

Weekend Chores Are Exhausting

Saturday:

Got up, first thing I did was drink big cups of coffee.

Then I went to the health club and did healthy stuff.

Then I went to doughnut world and did unhealthy stuff.

There's not really a big difference between healthy stuff and unhealthy stuff when you think about it.

Healthy stuff is good for you. Unhealthy stuff is good to you.

Next stop was the car dealership.

The distance between doughnut world and the car dealership is about three Boston creams – if you catch all the lights.

I can't swear this is what happened at the car dealership, because somehow I had come down with a major sugar high.

But this is how I remember it:

A salesman came over and asked me what it would take to put me in a car.

I told him Powerball. He said I could drive a car out with no money down.

I said the only way I could drive a car out was if it was no money period.

He said he would have to go talk to his boss. When he came back, he said his boss said it was a deal.

I said I'd think about it.

From the car dealership I went to Home Depot.

I love the smell of Home Depot in the morning. It smells like ... like ... tools.

In the paint department, I bought brushes and buckets and other things you need to paint a shed.

I also bought a gallon of paint, which was put on a nervous machine that made it jiggle like fat-guy breasts.

First thing I did when I got home was check out the shed.

There was good news. Only three sides needed to be painted because you can only see the fourth side in winter, and nobody's outside in the winter.

By the time I got everything ready to paint, it was time for lunch.

I'll tell you, you can really work up an appetite doing stuff around the house.

I was just about finished eating when I felt a nap coming on.

I figured my body was telling me something, so I listened.

While I was napping, I must have rolled on top of the TV remote, because when I woke up, the football game was on.

I didn't want to watch the game, but it was tied in the fourth quarter, so I really had no choice.

I was charged up to paint the shed after the game ended, but by that time it was getting dark. Some days you just can't catch a break, no matter how hard you work.

Sunday:

I slept late because Sunday is a day of rest, and I'm very religious about that.

Plus, I was still pretty beat from Saturday.

CHAPTER 9

DRIVING

Everyone out there is a moron — but me.

Road Rationing

It's funny where the great ideas come from.

Like one day you're idling in bumper-to-bumper land thinking about how the adjacent HOV lane should serve something resembling an actual purpose, when it hits you:

Floating Eyeballs Emergency Alleviation Corridor.

I mean, how many times have you been cruising along on the done side of an extra-large coffee only to encounter a dangerous backup – and we're not just talking traffic congestion here.

But this doesn't have to be. With absolutely no one using the barren lane next door, is there really any reason you need to be sitting there cross-legged and weeping?

No, in these situations you should be able to pull into the HOV lane and go for it. And you should not have to worry about being stopped for speeding or reckless driving or failure to display a mannequin.

But that's not the great idea.

It did, however, get me to thinking about how the highways are like the restrooms at hockey games. It's not that there aren't enough potties; it's that everyone wants to potty at once.

Which led me to the great idea – road rationing.

Think about it. We don't have too many motor vehicles in this country; we just all want to potty at the same time. (Revelations like this just give you chills, don't they?)

Anyway.

Although I am obviously more of a big-picture, big-concept kind of guy, I have put together a rough outline detailing how road rationing might work:

Commuters: People on the way to or from work will have the road from 6 to 9 a.m. and 4 to 7 p.m. During this time, no one else will be allowed on the road, except for emergency vehicles. But it will have to be a major emergency, one in which, say, the symptoms include rigor mortis.

Students: School buses will have the roads from 9 to 10 a.m. and 3 to 4 p.m. Granted, losing the opportunity to see how many vehicles they can stack up behind them will deprive drivers of a major job perk, but everyone has to sacrifice if this is going to work.

Seniors: It's all yours from 10 a.m. to 3 p.m. weekdays, no Saturdays and all day on Sunday. Early bird special waivers will be granted on a case-by-case basis.

Teenagers: Saturday nights until 11 if you are just going to be driving around, and till midnight if you are going to be parked in some secluded spot. (Note: For the midnight extension, boyfriends will need notarized waivers from girlfriends' fathers.)

Tractor-trailers: The right-back-at-ya set will be allowed to scare the bejesus out of each other from 8 p.m. to 6 a.m.

Pickup trucks: You people will be allowed on the road with cars, unless you start behaving like major-league apertures. If that happens, you will be reassigned to tractor-trailer hours, thereby becoming highway chum.

Delivery trucks: These vehicles can be driven on city streets during tractor-trailer hours but will not be allowed to stop unless they have a legal parking spot.

Construction equipment: Driving or moving construction equipment will only be permitted between midnight and 12:15 a.m. Because you bozos have really aggravated and inconvenienced us over the years, the penalty for disobeying the law will be fairly stern – lethal injection.

The Real Rules Of The Road

With the summer driving season upon us, this seems like a good time to review the Rules of the Road.

The Rules of the Road are, of course, different than traffic laws in that they reflect how we actually drive as opposed to how we are supposed to drive.

As a practical matter, it is much more important to know and understand and practice the Rules of the Road than it is to know and understand and obey traffic laws, which no one does anymore anyhow. Let's get started:

Changing lanes: The key thing to remember here is that surprise is your greatest ally, so never, ever signal. If you signal, you tip off drivers in the lane you wish to enter, thereby giving them the time to speed up so you can't enter.

Letting someone in: If you are in a line of traffic, and someone wishes to enter, do everything in your power to prevent them. Courtesy is a sign of weakness.

Tailgating: If we are all going to share the road, it seems only fair that we should also share each other's problems. So if you are late for work, or an appointment, or to pick up the kids, it is only right that you ride the rear bumper of any vehicle in your way, thereby making your problem their problem.

Speed limit: The posted speed limit should be taken for what it is – a minimum.

Intersections: If you wish to make a left turn at a four-way intersection, the correct procedure is to jump the green light and cut diagonally across in front of any oncoming traffic.

Traffic lights (What the colors mean):
> Green – Go.
> Yellow – Go.
> Red – Go.

Traffic signs (What they mean):
> Stop – Tap the brakes.
> Work Zone – Buzz the workers.
> Railroad Crossing – Beat the train.

Men in minivans: Men in minivans should be treated with care, kindness and understanding for the following reason: There but for the grace of God...

Road rage: It is perfectly normal to angrily pursue another driver right into his garage, regardless of what your therapist says.

Traffic backups: The correct thing to do if caught in a traffic jam is to use the breakdown lane to get ahead of as many people as possible.

SUVs: Might makes right (of way).

Cellphone etiquette: For dialing a number, use the left lane. For conversations that cause dramatic fluctuations in speed, use the center lane. For talking on a cellphone while also doing any of the following – eating, reading, typing, grooming or dozing – use any lane.

Happy motoring.

The Lost Art Of Parallel Parking

Waiting in traffic for a big guy to back a small car into a tight space: Parallel parking is a dying art.

It used to be that parallel parking was what separated the drivers from the aimers. People took pride in it. If you couldn't get a 16-foot car into a 17-foot spot on first try, you couldn't look yourself in the rearview mirror.

There were no multiple attempts – like this guy in front of me right now. You took your shot, and if you failed, you drove off, tailpipe between your legs.

Chances are the guy in front of me is from the suburbs.

I say this because people from the suburbs are the worst parallel parkers. Why?

Malls.

The malls, and the parking garage, are what killed parallel parking.

With their neat rows of lined spaces, they steadily chipped away at the craft, slowly reducing parking to the following three skills:

Pulling in.

Backing out.

Leaving enough room to open the doors.

People who live in cities can still parallel park. In fact, they are the finest parallelers to have ever dinged a bumper.

Most New Yorkers, for example, can wedge their car into a parking space without ever falling below the posted speed limit.

And they can do this while the cabbie behind is blaring his horn and people are sitting in the cars they are attempting to squeeze between.

Of course, drivers from the pre-power-steering era can also make a pretty good case for being the best ever.

I mean, if anyone ever calculated the calorie burn involved in parallel parking one of those manual-steering schooners from the '50s, we'd have the next workout-video craze on our hands.

The guy behind me gives the guy in front of me an aggravated toot. This additional pressure is more than the hacker can handle. He gives up and drives off.

I'm about to follow him up the street, when I think, what the heck.

I pull over, wave the people behind me around and put it in reverse.

Left hand on the wheel, right arm hooked around the seat, body twisted at the hips, neck craned to see out the rear window, I start backing in, steady, steady.

Instinctively, I cut the wheel, looking for the right angle. Not enough, and the tire digs into the curb; too much, and you're out in the middle of the street.

I slide the rear end in, and then turn my attention to the hood. I cut the wheel the other way – easy, easy – making sure my bumper doesn't touch the car in front.

Then, just as chrome clears chrome, I give the wheel a quick spin, hit the brake, throw it into drive, straighten out as I come forward, stick it into park, turn off the key and get out to assess my performance.

They say the great ones never lose it.

Plan B: Career In Road Obstruction

It is, of course, impossible to leave the driveway this time of year without immediately running into road construction.

Just why they call it construction is beyond me.

From my parking spot in the backup, the only thing I ever see being created is an opportunity to clean the glove compartment.

To be more accurate, road construction should not be called construction. It should be called obstruction.

Triangular signs should warn of obstruction zones, and traffic reporters should talk about obstruction delays, and people who work at these sites should be called obstruction workers.

Road obstruction, yeah, I could definitely work in this field.

Mind you, I'm not planning on going anywhere, but it's hard to feel secure about any job these days.

What with layoffs and buyouts and the ever-present temptation to quote noted proctologist Johnny Paycheck to the boss, you always need to be looking for your next gig.

If I ever did go into road obstruction, I think I would be best suited for one of the support positions – such as hole watcher.

Every obstruction site – by law, I believe – must be staffed by at least two guys who stand off to the side and stare into the hole.

Caution: Hole watchers should not be confused with shovel leaners or pickup-truck sitters.

I've considered these positions, too, but concluded I lack the coordination to be a shovel leaner and the ambition to become a pickup-truck sitter.

The other obstruction-site occupation I wouldn't be interested in is traffic god.

I mean, I might be drawn toward this calling if I were a police officer, because the way road obstruction works, police officers are only assigned if the obstruction is minimal or there is no traffic.

If, however, traffic is heavy and/or a complex intersection is involved, then traffic control is handled by a temporary worker undergoing on-the-job training in the intricacies of the Stop and Go paddle.

Anyway. There seem to be two classifications of hole watcher: senior hole watcher and entry-level hole watcher.

The senior hole watcher's main job is to tell the entry-level hole watcher when to jump into the hole.

Although a lot of people think the entry-level hole watcher jumps into the hole to perform some complex task, this is not the case.

The only reason he jumps into the hole is so the senior hole watcher can determine how deep it is.

For this reason, if you want to be an entry-level hole watcher, it's to your advantage to be of an even height. And I'm exactly 6 feet tall.

So, you know, I've got that going for me. Plus, orange is my color.

What Would Jesus Drive?

Brothers and Sisters, I come to you this morning with the word.

And the word this morning is not good, Brothers and Sisters, because the word this morning is blasphemy.

The General Motors Corp. is trying to use Jesus to sell its cars.

It is sponsoring an evangelical concert tour as part of a marketing campaign called "Chevrolet Presents: Come Together and Worship."

Selling heaven is not like selling automobiles, Brothers and Sisters.

In God's work, there is no zero-percent financing, no seven-year, 70,000-mile warranty, no trade-ins.

You can't stand up in front of the flock and ask sinners to drive, drag, push or tow their souls to the altar to be saved.

Jesus is many things, Brothers and Sisters, but a car salesman?

Close your eyes and try to picture it. Jesus, in a loud sports jacket, looking down on you and saying:

"What is it going to take to put you in this car today?"

The Lord works in mysterious ways, Brothers and Sisters, but not this mysterious.

Now, there are those who say that GM is crossing a line, blurring the divide between the commercial and the sacred. Church and state, they say, should not meet, and neither, I say, should church and Camaro.

The breach of this separation troubles me, Brothers and Sisters, but it is not what concerns me the most. The real desecration here, the blasphemy of blasphemes, is the implication that if Jesus were to return today, he would shine his light upon GM.

I don't claim to know everything, Brothers and Sisters, but I do know this: Jesus would not drive a Chevy.

Allah might drive a Chevy. Buddha might drive a Chevy. But you couldn't get Jesus in a Chevy no matter how good the deal.

So, then, what kind of car would Jesus drive?

I have reflected on this question, Brothers and Sisters, and I believe I have seen the way.

In my vision, I do not see Jesus in a Japanese car. I do not see Jesus in a Volvo, or a Beamer, or one of those Mercedes Benzes, though, praise the Lord, he would love those heated leather seats with winter coming.

Nor would Jesus drive a minivan, which is not to say he would not feel the suffering of the married men who bear such a cross.

And, certainly, Jesus wouldn't be caught resurrected in any of those gas-guzzling, road-hogging, conveyances of the devil himself, the SUVs.

No, Brothers and Sisters, when I look in my rear-view mirror I'll tell you what I see tailgating me.

I see a faded-blue, Ford F150 pickup with a tool box in the back, some minor body damage around the front fender and a vanity license plate that reads: Jesus. Can I have an amen?

Need Moron Specific Lanes

If you are driving on the highway, and you are going the speed limit, and you are using your signal lights, and you are not mindlessly drifting from lane to lane because you are eating or texting or cellphoning or reading the paper, then it means:

One, you are in the minority.

And, two, you aren't from around here.

Highway deaths and traffic mishaps may be down, but near hits and misses are accelerating. On any given day, the average highway driver now avoids more accidents than a 12-pack of Depends.

The problem isn't just all the distracted drivers. It's more that the growing ranks of distracted drivers now have to share the road with each other. This not only creates a dangerous situation for them, but also for those of us who are just trying to space out.

Enforcement is not the answer. Police have a hard enough time driving while talking on their own cellphones to concentrate on arresting people talking on theirs.

No, the solution I think rests in infrastructure. We need to redesign our highways to accommodate the increasing number of drivers who fail to take their attention spans along for the ride.

In my view, the best way to do this is with vastly wider highways featuring lanes dedicated to specific distractions.

Here are some options:

Texting lane: Rather than being straight, the lane lines would be wobbly to handle the drifting and weaving people typing with their thumbs.

Dining lane: Just a thought here, but maybe this lane might feature kind of a toll-booth setup where drivers could stop and grab a napkin before entering.

Reading lane: The most important consideration here, of course, would be to make sure there is good lighting.

Pet-on-lap lane: This lane would not only accommodate drivers with pets on their lap, but also pets with drivers on their laps. Don't laugh, I've seen it.

Moron lane: This would be reserved for drivers who are too dumb even to be allowed to mingle with the rest of the idiots in the various dope-specific lanes. It goes without saying that this would be the largest lane.

Driving In New York City

I had to drive into Manhattan this past week.

I was not carjacked.

I think it is important to note this, since gunpoint is the only way you could get most people behind the wheel in New York City.

It had been awhile since I'd driven in the city, so there was some pre-trip trepidation: some sweating, some shaking, some light vomiting. But no loss of bodily functions, which is usually a good omen.

Before embarking, I thoroughly checked the map. The only thing worse than driving in New York City is getting lost in New York City.

The directions included such well-traveled byways as the Hutch and the FDR. The route did not involve anything called Throgs Neck, much to my relief.

I've always had this uneasy thing about the Throgs Neck Bridge. I don't know what a throg is, or what a throg's neck looks like, and I have absolutely no desire to go over to its nesting place and find out.

We left early, but not early enough. If you get into the city before dawn, people are still out for the evening, and if you get there after it turns light, they're on their way to work. Kind of mimics the sleeping pattern of a college kid home for the summer.

As I exited the highway and entered the labyrinth, I tested my horn. I also reminded myself that under no circumstances should I use my turn signal. Signaling a turn in New York is taken as a sign of weakness.

The pregame jitters were still with me as I turned onto one of the busy avenues, but vanished as soon as the first yellow cab cut me off.

It was weird.

The more I drove, the more familiar and relaxed I felt. Then it hit me: New York City drivers didn't lack any more brain cells than Hartford-area drivers. Moron-wise, driving in New York was pretty much like driving around here.

I, of course, got lost trying to get out of town. Eventually, I finally found myself in sight of the highway ramp I need to be on, but on the wrong side of a busy intersection headed in the wrong direction.

I could have driven around some more looking for Mr. Right (turn), or I could have done what I did. Jump the light, bang an illegal U-eeee and head for the hills. The maneuver generated some fairly vigorous honking and gesturing, but it didn't bother me at all.

I knew it wasn't born of annoyance; it was born of admiration.

You Are What You Drive

I've been spending a lot of time sitting in traffic lately.

Some of the traffic has been holiday-related.

Some has been storm-related.

Some has just been everyday traffic, which is usually moron-related.

You get to know a lot of people when you're stuck in traffic.

Usually the encounters are visual, unless some slight is suffered, in which case they can become verbal, even digital.

In traffic, you are not who you are. In traffic, you are what you drive.

This is not as impersonal as it sounds, because who you are picks out what you drive.

The least popular people you meet in traffic are SUVs. SUVs are obnoxious, pushy and overbearing. Even people who are SUVs don't like SUVs. The SUV is the Simon Cowell of traffic.

Another unpopular person you meet in traffic are trucks.

These folks fall into two general categories:

Semis.

And pickups.

A semi is the guy you know from the bar who makes a lot of noise but no one asks to quiet down because he's big enough to sit in a booth and be surrounded by himself.

Although pickups have become more mainstream, overall they still tend to be bullies, line cutters, and mullets on wheels.

The Miss Congeniality of traffic is the Prius. Everybody loves the Prius. The Prius is cute, perky, polite and responsible. The Prius is also a tad on the smug and superior side, if you ask me. Most people are happy that others choose to be a Prius – so they don't have to be.

In traffic, you are not only what you drive but also how you drive.

People who drive too fast in traffic are %@*$%^$s.

People who drive too slowly in traffic are %@*$%^$s.

People who drive the speed limit are %@*$%^$s.

People driving directly behind you and directly in front of you, are real %@*$%^$s.

Traffic also has a class system. But it is not based on value or size. Rather, social rank is determined by the lane in which one drives.

Occupants of the right lane are the poor. No one even notices them.

The middle class, of course, occupies the middle lane, while the left lane is reserved for the folks on the fast track, the movers and shakers, the people who have places to go that are way more important than anyplace you have to be.

Finally, there is the breakdown lane. This is where the criminal class resides. People who drive in the breakdown lane are the American equivalent of untouchables, even if they are a Prius.

Slouching Drivers Are Slouches

Right off, let me be clear: I have nothing against short people.

I couldn't disagree more with Randy Newman when he sings: "Short people got no reason to live."

Of course, short people have a reason to live, if for no other reason than to populate the U.S. Senate.

The reason I mention short people is that, for a while there, I was convinced that the percentage of really short people driving cars had risen dramatically.

I based this driver-height observation on my morning commute, during which I seemed to have been coming up behind more and more vehicles that didn't appear to have anyone behind the wheel.

(For a while, I wondered it these cars were being operated by remote control in a quest for the ultimate multi-tasking stratagem: You stay home and send your car back and forth to work.)

The driverless car possibility was alarming, although only a little.

Given the aptitude of the average driver one encounters during the rush-hour commutes in these parts, I think a strong case can be made that a car being driven by no one is preferable to a car driven by someone.

Anyway.

As I passed these vehicles, I began to notice that most of those showing no visible hairline above the headrest were not little old ladies or folks propped up on pillows straining to see over the steering wheel.

Rather, these autos were being operated by younger men crouched down in the seat, with the back of their heads resting on the door at an angle, affording an unobstructed view of the sky and passing scenery. As for the road ahead ... eh.

On occasion I would see one of these low drivers sit up, and while he may not have risen to the heights of an NBA player, neither did he possess the physical stature of a senator.

Whatever is behind this new driving posture, I wish its devotees would understand just how much of a burden it places on other drivers.

There is really nothing more disconcerting – not to mention potentially threatening to one's well-being - than tailgating someone you believe to be a little old lady who turns out to be a slouching linebacker.

An Interstate Slice Of Life

The morning commute:

Too many cars.

Too little space.

Too much coffee.

You have these fantasies:

One involves a personal freeway.

One involves Power Ball.

One involves a monster truck with huge wheels that enables you to ride up over the cars in front of you and continue driving on their crushed roofs until you reach your exit leaving a pathetic pile of . . .

Anyway.

I'm cutting-in, cutting-off, and cursing-out my way to work, when I happen upon an always interesting slice of Interstate life – the traffic tiff.

Normally, when it comes to strangers' spats, I tend to side with the cheaper vehicle. I do this because I drive an old pickup truck – and because I'm petty.

In the drama currently unfolding, however, my rooting interest is not as clear-cut as usual because the protagonists are a Saab and a Beamer.

While this does sort of constitute a win-win situation from my warped perspective, it also removes a certain amount of entertainment value from the rapidly escalating encounter.

I am so bummed by this unfortunate turn of events that I am seriously considering changing lanes. Then I notice the bumper sticker on the back of the Beamer:

"Grow Your Own Dope, Plant a Man."

So now I have a favorite.

The Saab is being driven by an ordinary looking guy sporting a white shirt, blue tie and the standard reddish-purple commuter's complexion.

He has entered the oozing traffic from a left exit and ended up side-by- side with the Beamer. As the two vehicles inch along, the merge lane is steadily narrowing, meaning someone is going to have an attack of maturity fairly soon.

Finally, the guy in the Saab decides discretion is the better part of swapping paint with the Beamer.

He blinks.

But he doesn't let it go.

He allows the Beamer to get a few lengths ahead, and then accelerates quickly up behind it with his horn blaring, slamming on his anti-lock brakes at the very last second.

The woman in the Beamer responds by affording him a lengthy, rotating view of her middle finger.

As one might imagine, this has anything but a calming affect.

The scene is repeated a half dozen times or so over the next mile:

Blare. Brake. Salutation.

Blare. Brake. Salutation.

The two main characters in this motoring morality play become so engrossed in their bout of temporary insanity, that they are oblivious to everything else.

Neither notices when a six-wheel flatbed hauling a load of symbolism materializes beside them.

On the truck's back are two cement coffin vaults, one concrete gray, one spray painted gold. Linked and bound by chain, they quietly roll along side- by-side.

Who gets to go first doesn't seem to be an issue.

CHAPTER 10

THE JUNK DRAWER

Stuff that doesn't fit anywhere else like: Wal-Mart coffins and wakes for pets

Wal-Mart Coffins Stiff Competition

Giving new meaning to the term "box store," Walmart has begun selling coffins.

You can buy them online only.

One of the reasons you can't get them in stores is because they don't know what department to put them:

Bedding?

Outdoor living?

Gardening?

Walmart's 15-coffin line offers accommodations (single occupancy) beginning at $895 and ranging all the way up to $2,899 for the "Sienna Bronze." Other models include the "Regal Wide Body," the "American Patriot" and the pinstriped "Executive Privilege."

Given the aging baby-boomer market, other retailers are sure to follow Walmart's lead:

LL Bean: The retailer's top-of-the-line casket, "the Nor'easter," will appeal to its outdoor-minded clientele by offering a unit that can be used now and later. Simply pop out the removable fleece lining, and you have a rooftop luggage carrier. When it's time to go, slap the fleece back in, and you're good to go.

IKEA: For those who prefer a sleek, modern storage unit made from natural materials, how can you beat the Scandinavian furniture maker: ". . . isn't it good, Norwegian wood."

Ocean State Job Lot: Looking for a bargain? Don't mind a floor model, a fixer-upper or maybe a refurbished unit that was returned for some reason: leaked, wrong color, didn't fit? Then you've come to the right place.

Nieman-Marcus: The upscale retailer's top-of-the-line model, the grossly oversized "McCasket," will come in either silver or gold plating and include such amenities as fine Corinthian leather, heated pillow, Bose sound system and 24-hour concierge service.

McDonald's: Think the double-wide, plastic "Ronald McDonald Coffin," which can be filled with ice and soda and handed out as part of a promotional giveaway. And, yes, I'd want fries with that.

Bob's Discount Furniture: (I'm already hearing the commercials) Sure, you can spend $5,000 for a name-brand casket, or you can purchase Bob's "Boxapedic" for a fraction of the cost. So come on down.

Tupperware: Finally, for those who don't want to make a fuss when they go, what would be better than a long, clear, waterproof container that will be airtight for eternity ... as long as the funeral director remembers to burp the corner.

Sending Off Dearly Departed Dogs

Formal services for pets are becoming more common.

What we are talking about here are calling hours, funerals, burials in exclusive pet cemeteries.

Does this strike anyone else as being just a little . . . much?

I don't mean to be insensitive here. I've been owned by dogs all my life. I understand the loss. I understand how a pet can be a family member, a loving friend, a trusted confidant.

I don't understand how they can become heirs to $12 million, but then I've always underestimated the power of sucking up.

That said:

I find the idea of attending a pet wake more than just a bit unsettling.

How would it work?

Would there be an open casket and, if so, how would Old Sparky be laid out?

On his side like he was sleeping?

Standing on his hind legs with a ball or Frisbee in his mouth?

Sitting up smiling and offering a paw?

Would I be expected to go alone, or bring my dog if he was friends with Old Sparky?

What if my dog saw Old Sparky sitting up and smiling and had an accident?

What if I saw Old Sparky sitting up and smiling and had an accident?

When our turn came at the casket, would it be OK if my dog gave Old Sparky's butt a final sniff?

Would it be disrespectful if I skipped this protocol?

What about the services – would they be denominational?

By that I mean, would Irish Setters be Catholic and English Sheep Dogs Episcopalian? If so, what would, say, a Labradoodle be, Unitarian?

Some other questions:

How will people know if a pet has passed away. Will there be pet obituaries?

In terms of condolences, would you send flowers or treats?

At the graveside service, would you cry or howl?

What would you say to the deceased's owner. "He's in a better place now."

Do all pets go to heaven?

What happens if your pet goes to heaven and you don't?

If dogs participate in the actual funeral, will they be called pawbearers?

Would the pawbearers ride in the hearse on the way to cemetery, or chase it?

Obviously, much remains to be worked out.

Is My Love Life Normal?

"Are You Normal About Sex, Love and Relationships?" the book title asks. I doubt it, I figure, but I can't say for sure.

So I sharpen a No. 2 pencil, sit up straight and try to answer questions posed in the book:

Q: Do you think there is only one person out there for you?
A: No, but I'm pretty sure my wife does.

Q: Do you [and your spouse] wear each other's clothes?
A: Depends on the laundry situation.

Q: Do you think sex improves with age?
A: Whose age are we talking about here?

Q: Is love blind?
A: As I recall, it can be if you have been drinking.

Q: What is your most common sexual fantasy?
A: It involves Betty White, a set of Michelin radials, and a spatula.

Q: Do you fret that your sexual fantasies aren't normal?
A: Why would I?

Q: Do you think about sex on the way to work?
A: Mostly I think about killing cellphone users on the way to work.

Q: What is the most romantic movie you ever saw?
A: Gotta go with "Chitty Chitty Bang Bang."

Q: How long did you plan your wedding?
A: Personally, about 10 minutes.

Q: What did you argue about most with your partner while planning your wedding?
A: Why we had to invite her relatives.

Q: Did you toss your garter?
A: Nope, I still have it on.

Q: Have you ever tossed rice?
A: No, but on many occasions I have tossed cookies.

Q: Are you affected by PMS?
A: Nah, I just tune everything out.

Q: What disturbs you most when you are nude in front of your partner?
A: The dark.

Q: Do you carry around your pet's photo?
A: This is getting kinky, but yeah.

Q: Have you ever had Chlamydia?

A: No, but I had a Lhasa apso when I was a kid.

Q: Would you dress more revealingly to double your salary?
A: Are you kidding? I'd wear a thong for an extra 10 bucks a week.

Q: Would you sell your spouse for a million dollars?
A: I'd need to see something in writing.

Q: What if your partner turned passive during sex?
A: You mean like snoring? I hate when that happens.

Q: Would you rather watch football or have sex?
A: I'd rather watch sex and have football.

Q: Do you think giving a gift [on Valentine's Day] will increase your chances of getting sex?
A: Do I look like I just fell off the turnip wagon?

The Real Cruelest Month

January is not a month.
It is:
A mood.
A mode.
A test.
In days, January totals 31.
In dog years, January runs seven months.
In reality, January is forever.
To survive January one must possess:
Mettle.
Determination.
Chocolate.
To go with the chocolate:
A couch.
A clicker.
A Blockbuster.
People who make resolutions in January,
People who go on diets in January,
People who look beyond the moment in January,
Are fools.
January is not about self-improvement, it's about survival.
The following people were born in January:
Mozart.
Gretzky.
Ali.
FDR.
MLK.
Elvis.
The following people were most likely conceived in January:
Fran Drescher.
Ricki Lake.
Charlie Sheen.
Adam Sandler.
Someone named Dweezil.
There is a message in this.
Normally, January has two types of weather:
Atrocious.
Atrociouser, which is not really a word, unless you live in New England.
January also produces:
A thaw, which is known locally as the January incubation.
People have mixed feelings about the January incubation.
On the one hand, it often produces near-death chest colds.

On the other, it cuts down on the frostbite.

There is no sense of fashion in January.

Those who attempt to dress stylishly in January risk being spit out of a glacier intact 4,000 years from now.

Proper January attire is limited to:

Flannel.

Fleece.

Down.

Fur.

Sweat pants.

It is difficult, if not impossible, to look cool in January.

One reason is lack of sunglasses time.

In January, the sun shines only long enough to resurface the black ice.

Fancy, flashy cars do not do well in January.

Basic, boxy, four-wheel drives do.

The best car to have in January?

A Zamboni.

January does have one redeeming quality.

It's not February.

The Mind Wanders

Tossing and turning at 3 a.m.:

I'd get up and go if it wasn't so cold.

Wonder how much it costs every time the furnace goes on?

Wonder if I can hold it for another three hours?

If a bladder explodes and no one hears it, does it still make a sound?

Virgin Atlantic Airways, can you believe those guys?

They were actually surprised people objected to their plans to install bright-red urinals shaped like women's open lips at JFK.

Talk about clueless.

Best design for a urinal – a target.

Uh-oh, still have that version of "White Rabbit" stuck in my head:

"One pill makes you larger,

"And no pill keeps you small,

"And the ones that mother gives you,

"Don't do anything at all.

"Go ask Cialis.

"When it's 10 feet tall."

You know, I should have gone into advertising. ...

"Tell 'em a hooka-smoking caterpillar has given you the call ..."

Enough!

Maybe I should look at the clock to see if the time has changed.

Maybe I'm asleep.

Maybe I'm just dreaming about being awake.

Or maybe I'm having a dream about having a dream about being awake.

Sleeping didn't used to be this complicated.

3:15 a.m., darn. I knew I shouldn't have looked.

Where did I read that members of the 50-ish set are holding colonoscopy parties?

I guess it's a mutual support thing. You get a group of friends to schedule colonoscopy exams at the same time.

Wonder what you do at the party?

You can't eat.

You can't drink.

And playing Twister would definitely be out.

I suppose you could just talk.

Phrases you should avoid at a colonoscopy party:

Got hosed.

The whole nine yards.

In the pink.

I'll bet Martha Stewart is awake.

Let me see if I can reach her: Marrrrrrtha. Marrrrrrtha. She's not picking up. The telepathic service here is lousy.

You know, I could replace Martha:
Duct tape crafts.
Deep-fat-fried holidays.
I need to get an agent.
Wonder what time it is now?
Maybe I'll just get up.
But what if I'm asleep?
If I'm asleep and I get up, it could wake me up, and then I'll never get back to sleep.
3:30 a.m.
Only 2 1/2 hours to go.
"And if you go chasing rabbits ..."
Oh, no.

Doctor's Questionnnaire

(To be filled out by patient's physician prior to treatment.)

Personal:
First Name (other than "Doctor").
Address (list all homes).
Phone (home, business, beeper, car, golf cart).
Handicap.
Mercedes or BMW?
Besides medical-ese, do you speak any other languages?

Education
Where did you go to medical school?
Is this medical school in the Caribbean?
List the medical schools that rejected you. (Use the back if you need more space.)
What was your class rank?
Out of how many?
List all subjects in which you didn't get an A.
How often did you cut classes to go to the beach?
What was your worst subject?
Is this an area in which you will be treating me?

Professional
(If you are not a surgeon, skip to next section.)
Aside from the money, why did you choose surgery?
Who carves the Thanksgiving turkey in your house?
Speaking of fowl, if a duck quacks, do you ever say "what"?
How many times during the day do you use the word "oops"?
Do morticians send you birthday cards?
Have you ever had any of the following nicknames: Shaky, Spaceman, Spaz or Code Red?

Insurance
Name of primary malpractice-insurance carrier.
Are you in the risk pool?
Do people in the claims department recognize your voice?
Are you uncomfortable around people named Sue?
Does your coverage include liability and incision?

Appointments
How many patients do you ordinarily schedule for the same time?
In general, do you see the cramming of sick people into a small space for long

periods of time as being a good way to maintain inventory?

How long is too long for a patient to be kept waiting?

In the entire time you have been practicing medicine, have you ever run ahead of schedule?

Have you ever played 18 between patients?

How about 9?

When was the last time you changed your magazines?

(When you are done, please return this form to the receptionist, and have a seat. The patient will be with you as soon as possible.)

An Inconvenient Truth

I didn't believe this when I first heard it, but apparently cows are major contributors to global warming.

Seems they emit big-time amounts of methane gas.

Some studies estimate that cows and other livestock are responsible for as much as 18 percent of the gases that cause warming.

This means that in many places they are producing more harmful gases than automobiles, airplanes and fraternity brothers.

If this is true, the obvious question is how do they know this? How do you – besides very carefully – measure cow flatulence?

I suppose you could stand behind old Bessie with a large garbage bag or something and attempt to capture the back draft when it occurs.

The problem with this methodology is that it is hit or miss (possibly literally), and not very time efficient.

A better way might be to study cow behavior. For example, do cows make faces or maybe lift one leg off the ground before firing?

Another approach could focus on identifying those cows who – like their human counterparts – view the natural emission process as not only a form of entertainment but self-expression.

How hard would it be to pick out the weird uncle cows – you know, the ones who are always walking up to the calves and saying, "Here, pull my hoof."

How difficult would it be to isolate cows who after cutting loose immediately attempt to blame it on somebody else?

Besides the actual collection process, you also have to wonder about the people doing the collecting.

Is this one of those things they always wanted to be ever since they could remember?

Is it a recognized profession?

Is it something you go to school for?

What are you called?

And just what do you tell the other person on a first date when they inquire about your occupation:

"So what do you do for a living?"

"I'm in bovine expulsion collection and data analysis."

"You measure cow farts! Check."

The solution to this warming problem may be as uncomplicated as neutralizing the pollution at the source.

Perhaps cows could be fitted with some type of catalytic converters.

Or maybe massive amounts of Beano could be added to their diets.

Then again, maybe all that needs to be done is to get some frat brothers to teach them to use cigarette lighters.

Looking For Afterlife Loopholes

I have just been reading an AARP survey about life after death.

I don't know if I believe in life after death, but I'm definitely for it.

The survey involved 1,000 people age 50-plus.

Seventy-three percent of those polled said they believed in life after death, and 66 percent said their belief got stronger as they got older.

This is not surprising.

When W.C. Fields, a lifelong atheist, was dying, his nephew walked into the acerbic comedian's hospital room one day and found him reading the Bible.

"Uncle, what are you doing!" he asked.

Replied Fields, "Looking for loopholes."

Another way of looking at it, I guess, is the closer you get to the end of the party, the more important it becomes to find an after-hours joint.

Anyway, in terms of a destination, 86 percent of respondents said they believe in heaven, while 70 percent said they believe in hell.

I'm concerned that so many people believe in hell. What if they're right? What if there is such a place? I wouldn't mind the heat so much as long as it isn't humid.

Another thing in the survey that kind of bothers me is that while 88 percent of those who believe in heaven think they are going there, they also think only 64 percent of the rest of us will be joining them.

I'm kind of surprised by this assessment.

I always thought hell was reserved for those who have done something really, really unforgivable, like, say, Bill Buckner.

Not everyone questioned in the survey believed one's options upon death were either up or down. Twenty-three percent said they believed in reincarnation, a figure that grew to 31 percent in the Northeast.

I've always liked the idea of coming back to earth, although ideally I'd like to have some input into what I return as. I mean, if I'm going to come back as a slug or a politician, forget it.

If I had my choice, I wouldn't mind being reincarnated as a backup singer for a group like the Temptations.

Another thing the survey found was that 60 percent of women and 40 percent of men believe in spirits or ghosts. Not only that, but 38 percent of respondents said they have felt the presence of something that they thought might have been a spirit or ghost.

I've had that kind of feeling myself from time to time, but I always figured it was the government.

Finally, 77 percent of survey participants said they are not frightened by what happens after they die. When the time comes, I think I'm going to hang out with these folks.

In the meantime, I'll continue looking for loopholes.

Proper Cleavage Etiquette

The last time I wrote about this subject, I got grief.

What I said was that men watch the Academy Awards for only two reasons – cleavage.

Times have changed. Cleavage has gone mainstream. These days cleavage is like motorcycles; they're everywhere.

Public cleavage was once reserved for specific social occasions like fancy cocktail parties where the highlight is stabbing little wieners with toothpicks. In contrast, there now is no such thing as a cleavage-free zone, no escaping the great divide.

Cleavage has also become controversial. Hillary Clinton once created a bit of a stir by showing showing up on the Senate floor in pants, a pink jacket, black blouse and cleavage. This prompted a fashion writer from the Washington Post to criticize the quality of Clinton's cleavage, writing: "It was more like catching a man with his fly unzipped. Just look away!"

Obviously, the Post fashion writer was a woman. To the male, there is no such thing as "look away" cleavage.

Which is not to suggest that all cleavage is created equal.

It isn't.

You have your common cleavage, your above-average cleavage, your overachieving cleavage and your "Star Trek" cleavage, which has the power to take men where no man has gone before.

Then you have your long cleavage, your stubby cleavage, your wide-body cleavage, your shallow cleavage, your mesa cleavage, your shy cleavage, your full-disclosure cleavage, your full-contact cleavage, your pumped-up cleavage and your reined-in cleavage yearning to breathe free.

Age-wise, there's your late-model cleavage, your middle-age cleavage, your senior cleavage and your vintage cleavage, which is sometimes referred to as "over-the-hills" cleavage.

All of which is suitable for viewing, with one exception: male cleavage. Male cleavage is always "look away" cleavage, unless, that is, you happen to find Jell-O with hair on it appealing.

With cleavage having become so up-front, it might be a good idea at this point to review some basic cleavage etiquette:

1.) Is it proper to compliment someone on their cleavage? Certainly, but keep it simple: "I love your cleavage."

2.) Should you thank someone for providing cleavage? Absolutely, but again, less is better: "Thank you for the cleavage; I really appreciate it."

3.) Is it OK to stare at cleavage? The short answer is yes, but within limits. A good rule of thumb is that it is acceptable to behold until you blink, at which point politeness dictates you make eye contact with the presenter.

Down Dog With A Dog

There are a lot of things you can do with a dog.

Yoga isn't one of them.

After reading how something called "Doggie Yoga" is the new big thing out on the West Coast, I thought I would give it a try with my dog Harry.

I should have known better.

After rolling out my mat and taking off my shoes, I woke up Harry. There aren't a lot of things you do with Harry that don't involve waking him up first.

I figured I would start off with something easy, something Harry could relate to, a yoga posture called down dog.

After demonstrating the movement several times, I told Harry to give it a try. He came over, looked at the mat and licked my face.

I went through the whole thing again, patiently offering little tips about paw placement and hip angle.

Harry watched me intently, then rolled onto his side and licked himself.

This made me think that if dogs are going to do yoga with people, dogs really need to wear pants.

I went back and read the "Doggie Yoga" story again.

"Don't be too ambitious," the instructor advised. "Honor your dog, and remember, they respond to our energy."

I summoned up all the energy and honor at my disposal and slowly walked Harry through the pose one more time. When I was done, he looked at me and yawned.

I closed my eyes for several minutes and drew deep breaths. While I was doing this, I could also hear Harry starting to breathe deeply. Hey, he's catching on, I thought.

When I opened my eyes, Harry looked very centered, very focused, very at peace. Then I realized he was asleep. I started chanting "neuter, neuter, neuter." That woke him up.

I considered teaching Harry to breathe through his nose, but I thought better of it. When dogs breathe through their nose, a lot of wet stuff comes out.

By this point, I was having serious reservations about "Doggie Yoga," which were reinforced when Harry rolled over on his back and stretched out all four legs.

There is truly not a more unattractive sight in the world than a dog on its back with its legs stretched out.

I was about to pack it in when Harry nonchalantly sat up, put one of his legs behind his head and scratched his ear. Then he reached his head back toward his tail, while giving me a look that said `let's see you do this,' and gave his business end a sniff.

For me, that was the last straw.

There is no place in yoga for show-offs.

Jim Shea - The Man

Jim Shea was born and educated in Waterbury, where he earned the distinction of being one of the few people who the nuns could not teach to spell. Save for college, and two unfortunate weeks in law school, he has lived in Connecticut all his life. He is married with two daughters, and has worked at the Courant for 27 years, including stints as a sports writer and lifestyle general assignment reporter. In 1996 he wrote a book about UConn basketball called "Huskymania." These days he writes three humor columns a week, produces a blog called TooShea, and appears in a weekly TV commentary for Fox CT. In his spare time he goes to the gym, runs some, cycles, and practices yoga, where he routinely exhibits the flexibility of a bureaucrat. He also spends a lot of time on couch patrol watching the Red Sox. Where does he get his ideas? His wife claims "Merlot."

Acknowledgements

Special thanks to the array of talented people at
CT1 Media who made this book possible including
Courant Editor Naedine Hazell, who edited the book;
Director of Graphics and Design Chris Moore, who
designed it; Graphic Designer Wes Rand, who did
the illustrations; Courant Photographer Steve Dunn;
the Courant's copy desk; Communications Strategist
Andrea Savastra, who oversaw the publishing; and
Vice President of Creative Services and Marketing
Joseph Schiltz, who agreed to take on this project.
Also, special thanks to my wife, Jan, whose input
was invaluable.

In Memory

Skip LeMonnier and Charlie Hibbert,
friends lost along the way.

CPSIA information can be obtained at www.ICGtesting.com
261842BV00002B/1/P

9 780615 423845